THINKING ANIMALS

Thinking Animals

WHY
ANIMAL
STUDIES
NOW?

Kari Weil

COLUMBIA UNIVERSITY PRESS

NEW YORK

Columbia University Press
Publishers Since 1893
New York   Chichester, West Sussex
cup.columbia.edu
Copyright © 2012 Columbia University Press
All rights reserved
Library of Congress Cataloging-in-Publication Data
Weil, Kari.
Thinking animals : why animal studies now? / Kari Weil.
p. cm.
Includes bibliographical references (p.   ) and index.
ISBN 978-0-231-14808-5 (cloth : alk. paper) —
ISBN 978-0-231-14809-2 (pbk. : alk. paper) —
ISBN 978-9-231-51984-7 (ebook)
1. Animals (Philosophy) 2. Animals in literature.
I. Title.
B105.A55W45   2012
113'.8—dc23   2011035566

For

Michael,

Sophie,

and the animals

we've loved

One thing is necessary above all if one is to practice reading as an *art*. Something for which one has almost to be a cow and in any case *not* a modern man: *rumination.*

—Friedrich Nietzsche, *Genealogy of Morals*,
trans. Walter Kaufmann

CONTENTS

CONTENTS

ACKNOWLEDGMENTS

This book would not have been written without the vision and support of Wendy Lochner at Columbia University Press, and my first thanks go to her for encouraging me to write it and for wanting to include me in her growing list of authors in animal studies.

I first came to understand the exciting possibilities and widening interdisciplinary parameters of the field of animal studies at the annual conferences for the Society for Literature, Science, and the Arts. Richard Nash was, I believe, the first to organize a stream of "animal panels" for these conferences, and I am indebted to him and to society members Ron Broglio, Susan Squier, and Susan McHugh for including me in panels and publications and for enlivening the conversation around the representations of nonhuman animals. I also thank Teresa Mangum, Jane Desmond, and Nigel Rothfels for inviting me to participate in the 2007 "Animal Agenda" and for the fascinating discussions we had regarding efforts to integrate academic research in animal studies with public engagement. I am grateful to my previous institution, the California College of the Arts, and to Wesleyan University for allowing me to teach courses in what was not yet known as "animal studies" and to my students in the courses "Thinking Animals" and "Animal Subjects" at both institutions for the seriousness and excitement of their efforts in and outside of class. I also thank the Humane Society of the United States for choosing my California

College of the Arts course "Animal Subjects" to receive the Best Established Course Award for 2006: its recognition was meaningful for me personally and for the field of animal studies more generally.

At Wesleyan University, I have been privileged to have Lori Gruen as a colleague and collaborator on a variety of animal projects, beginning with "Who's Looking?"—a collaborative investigation of human relations to chimpanzees that included Frank Noelker's exhibited exhibition Chimp Portraits. Lori's expertise in ethics has been as instructive for me as our work and dinners together have been inspirational. I am also grateful to my department, the College of Letters, for freeing me to participate as a fellow at Wesleyan's Center for the Humanities in the fall semester of 2008 and to the center's director, Jill Morawski, and the other fellows for our lively and provocative discussions. Andrew Curran offered a particularly helpful and responsive ear during the semester, and I thank him for his continuing interest in and engagement with my work. I also thank him for introducing me to Thierry Houquet, who invited me to submit an essay for his special issue of the French journal *Critique* on animal liberation. That essay would become part of this book's penultimate chapter, and I also presented it at the Animals and Society Institute, where I was a peer scholar during the summer of 2009. I am grateful to the institute's directors, Ken Shapiro and Margo de Mello, for inviting me; to Kathy Rudy, who hosted the institute that summer; and to the other fellows and participants for their enthusiastic response to my work.

My final thanks go to Michael and Sophie, to whom this book is dedicated. From courting me on horseback and allowing our dogs on the bed to taking it in stride as my habits of eating and cooking changed over the course of writing this book, Michael has indulged me in my creaturely cravings and in many instances has even come to share them. As for Sophie, having grown up with a flurry of tails and tales, she has taught me much about the differences and similarities among the various members of our family and reminds me how important it is to love each one attentively and with endless appreciation for the love they return.

Some of the material here was previously published in journals, which have graciously offered permission to reproduce my work.

Chapter 1 originally appeared as "A Report on the Animal Turn," *differences* 21, no. 2 (Summer 2010): 1–23.

Part of chapter 7 appeared in a slightly different version as "Killing Them Softly: Animal Death, Linguistic Disability, and the Struggle for Ethics," *Configurations* 14, nos. 1–2 (2006): 87–96.

An earlier version of chapter 8 first appeared in French as "Liberté ehonté," "Libérer les animaux?" a special issue of *Critique* 747–748 (August–September 2009): 664–677. A later version appeared as "Shameless Freedom," *JAC* 30, nos. 3–4 (2010): 713–726.

INTRODUCTION

"An animal looks at us and we are naked before it. Thinking, perhaps, begins there."[1] These two lines from Jacques Derrida's *The Animal That Therefore I Am* have been much cited even as they remain elusive and haunting. What does it mean that thinking begins in the confrontation between human and nonhuman animal? What is this thinking that has not been thought before or that has not been thought by the philosopher before? And what is this nakedness to which the encounter with an animal (an individual animal and not "the animal" or the concept of animality) returns us? Does a confrontation with and acknowledgment of another animal expose us as humans by stripping us of those clothes and thinking caps with which we have claimed to stake our difference from animals? If so, how and why, as Derrida goes on to say, does he and/or the philosopher experience shame in this nakedness before his cat?

Since Aristotle, man (as used in most texts) has been defined as the "rational animal," distinguished from other animals by his (and, more recently, her) ability to think and to reason. But this distinctive property has come under much questioning in recent years as we learn almost daily how many other species do something that appears to be thinking—whether in the ways they prepare their nests or hide their food or court their mates. One wonders if it is in anticipation of such discoveries that in his essay "What Is Called Thinking?" (1954),

Martin Heidegger professed that we, humans, have not yet really begun to think, that we have not thought in the ways that only our humanity can allow for. Heidegger was critical of the distinction of "rational animal" because it insisted too much on animality as the basis for human rationality.[2] The phrase, he believed, discounts the qualitative difference of our ability to know and relate to the world around us—even if we have not always seized the full potential of thought. Writing against Heidegger's brand of humanism, Derrida claims that the kind of thinking that has not been done and that has become all the more urgent to do is a thinking that happens through recognition and acknowledgment of the animals we are and with whom we share our world.

Bêtise, which is most often translated as "stupidity," is a word that Derrida uses to describe the kind of knowledge that excludes real thinking. It is a word he takes from the nineteenth-century French author Gustave Flaubert (among others), whose novel *Bouvard and Pécuchet* illustrates the particular stupidity of attempting to master the world through a cataloging of knowledge. "La Bêtise," wrote Flaubert in a famous letter, "consists in wanting to conclude."[3] Of course, what is especially intriguing in this word that is derived from the French word for beast (*bête*) is that it refers to a kind of beastly stupidity that is proper to humans. "The animal," Derrida reminds us, "cannot be *bête*."[4] According to the distinctions we humans make between animals and ourselves, animals cannot be stupid in this way. Is this why real thinking must begin in or through our confrontation with the look of animals, through their gaze upon us and upon the world, a gaze that ignores our conclusions? "The best literature," Derrida writes, citing Gilles Deleuze, "lets itself be 'haunted' by *bêtise*, haunted by the problem of *bêtise*."[5] It is that haunting in literature as well as in the visual arts, philosophy, and theory that is the focus of this book insofar as it results from our encounters with animals and our relations with them. Our engagement with animals may reveal to us our particular human stupidity, and it is only by deeply attending to animals or, more precisely, by becoming "attuned" to them, I want to suggest, that we may be able to think otherwise and overcome some of the limitations of our so-called rational condition.

Claude Lévi-Strauss wrote that animals are "good to think,"[6] but my book's premise is that it is good to "unthink" animals and so to rethink our conclusions about who we are, who they are, and how we all are intertwined. Donna Haraway uses the word *entanglement* to speak of the inseparability of human and nonhuman worlds and of the "naturecultures" that have evolved as a result.[7] Derrida's term *heteroaffection*, or the way that the self is touched or moved by an other, takes on a similar valence when he uses it in relation to animals. His book *The Animal That Therefore I Am* exposes the false autonomy of his thinking self that has been moved by his cat's gaze and thus feels, often to his dismay, the cat stirring and stirring within. The narratives and artworks I address here also reveal or attempt to come to grips with the animals that get inside of us. As a consequence, they demand a kind of "unthinking" from their keepers and viewers. To be sure, the demand to unthink or to destabilize our conceptual categories has been especially associated with postmodernism, but only some of the works I treat here are postmodern. Modernism shares with postmodernism a sense of the inadequacy of Enlightenment categories for knowing the world and representations of animals, and our engagements with them have brought this inadequacy to the fore in both movements. What may be different in modernism and postmodernism, however, is the act of representation itself and how the act of representation may or may not be a part of the problem of understanding and responding to our entanglements.

It would appear that modernism (or at least the modernist works I treat here), even in its turn to animals, relies on a greater degree of conceptual coherence and distinction in its representation of such categories as "man," "woman," "dog," "cat," "life," "death"—representations that clearly borrow from realism—with the result that it appears to be grounded in the very humanism that has authored those categories. Such is this humanism, moreover, that it has denied ethical standing to animals while assuring the exceptionalism of the human condition. But in most cases this coherence also results in a clearer ethical or political affiliation and agenda insofar as there are distinct identities; in modernism, we know (or believe we can determine) who is acting, who is acted upon, what is right, what is wrong, and who consequently is to be condemned for wrong actions. Postmodernist works, in their enthusiastic disruption of identities and breaking down of boundaries, often seem to give up the ethical to an anarchic thrill. They do important work by bringing us into the thick of our entanglements, of our irreducible heteroaffections and infections. But they make it difficult to determine what, if any, our responsibilities are for and to those relations. By moving between modernist and postmodernist works, I respond to the request that Haraway made many years ago in her cyborg essay to take "pleasure in the confusion of boundaries and the responsibility in their construction."[8] Indeed, I hope to go further than merely taking "pleasure in confusion" in order to show the urgency of undoing those boundaries between human and animal. Derrida, like Giorgio Agamben, writes of the violence produced by categories such as "the animal" that are used to separate humans from what they are not and to establish and justify our dominance. The ultimate violence may result from the kind of thinking that concludes that there are beings against whom it is impossible to commit a crime—in other words, that there can be no crimes against animals, only against humans. But it is unclear to me whether the remedy for such violence is, as Agamben seems to suggest, a "Shabbat of both animal and man"[9] or abandonment of such distinctions rather than taking on the full responsibility for the construction of such distinctions.

The writing of this book began with a haunting of my own. I was haunted by J. M. Coetzee's novel *Disgrace*. I began to write about this book as a way to understand why it was so upsetting and why I could not get it out of my mind. That writing went through a number of versions, some of which are now parts of chapters 7 and 8. I had already begun to write about animal subjects, mostly about women and gender and horses in nineteenth-century France—work I am still pursuing. *Disgrace* brought issues of gender, race, and animals together in a way that I had not yet experienced and could not get my mind around. To be sure, feminists such as Carol Adams and Josephine Donovan have illustrated and theorized how oppressions of gender, race, and species are interlocking, and their work has been groundbreaking.[10] In the way *Disgrace* affected me, it seemed both to support such theories and in the end to render them inadequate. Surprisingly, if not perversely, the very male protagonist appears to make amends for his own acts of violence and to discover the power of true love—love worthy of its name—in the company of animals and in the act of killing them.

As is my way when I come up against such a difficulty and perversion in thinking that the best of literature produces, I look for clarification in other works, usually theoretical or philosophical. The oppositional way of thinking that fiction (or poetry) and philosophy promote is one that Coetzee himself thematizes in his book *The Lives of Animals*, as if to suggest that some sort of dialectic between the two may be necessary at times for recognizing the pains and pleasures of others—especially other animals—and simultaneously for finding ways to respond to the ethical and political dilemmas they present. Thus, I move in this book not only between modernist and postmodernist works, but also between works of art (literary and visual) and works of philosophy (or theory), even if at times the one kind of thinking may appear to haunt the other or arise from its core. Divided into four parts, the book thus begins by focusing on questions of theory and philosophy (with the aid of literature and visual art), moves to literary readings (read through or against philosophy and theory), and ends with a combination of both. More specifically, the first part focuses on why animal studies has become important for theory and philosophy; the second and third examine a few exemplary modernist and postmodernist fictions of the ways we live with animals and the ways they live and die with us and often under our command; the fourth weaves themes broached in the first two in an effort to think through some of the ethical stakes of our theories and our fictions alike. French, German, British, Russian, and American, these texts spring from even as they write against our Western literary and cultural heritage regarding human–animal relations. I have chosen these texts not because they promote a common ethical stance—except insofar as they pay close attention to nonhuman animals, which is remarkable in itself—but because they illustrate the difficulties of arriving at such a stance. Ethical considerations, as Barbara Herrnstein Smith writes, are the product of historical and social example, shaped "by the approval or disapproval of other people, at least those we see as our own kind," as well as by individual, "critical reflection."[11]

Part I—"Why Animal Studies Now?"—is divided into two chapters. The first, "A Report on the Animal Turn," examines the recent rise of animal studies in the academy and the critical shifts that have made the question of the animal a central issue for theory. Here I suggest that theory's turn to animals grows out of, on the one hand, a weariness with post-structuralism's linguistic turn and a resulting search for a postlinguistic and perhaps posthuman sublime and, on the other hand, an often conflicting turn to ethics that raises the question of our human responsibility to the animal–other. The theoretical issues raised in this chapter are illustrated through a reading of Franz Kafka's 1917 story "A Report to an Academy" and are also disturbed by the story's ape-turned-human, whose account of his life shores up theory's blind spots. The second chapter, "Seeing Animals," couples core philosophical arguments surrounding the nature or being of animals and the grounds on which they may or may not be granted subjectivity, using two documentary artists' efforts to make visible what might be called the very being of animals. Moving from Heidegger's and Jakob von Uexküll's writings on animal worlds to Thomas Nagel's "What Is It Like to Be a Bat" and Derrida's *The Animal That Therefore I Am*, I chart the persistent desire to know what it is like to be an animal (especially the "animal I am") and the way this desire is frustrated by our means of apprehending and representing such knowledge. This frustration is announced in the title of Bill Viola's *I Do Not Know What It Is I Am Like*, a video that, I argue, strives for an aesthetics of "attunement," to borrow Heidegger's term for a capacity to be affected or tuned by that of which we have no knowledge, but that is common to all animal life, human and nonhuman. Whereas Viola's attempt to capture this animal likeness that we long to know but cannot see might be characterized as a "posthumanist posthumanism," photographer Frank Noelker's contrasting "humanist posthumanism" captures and makes visible the humanity of our fellow animals, especially chimpanzees.[12] In his photographic exhibition Chimp Portraits, I argue, Noelker makes use of what I call a strategic or critical anthropomorphism that turns chimps' "human" gaze back upon us to make us question how well we know who or what is human. Perhaps this is why Derrida suggests that thinking begins in the confrontation with an animal who looks at us.

Part II, "Pet Tales," begins with an overview of theories regarding our most common form of interaction with live animals in industrial societies—the institution of pet keeping. In an essay from 1980 that has become a classic of animal studies, entitled "Why Look at Animals,"

John Berger grouped pet keeping with zoos and other institutions whereby we try to regain a closeness to animals that we have lost in our modern, industrialized world but in the end imprison them in an artificial way of life that demands their deanimalization. Berger's views are echoed in the theories of "becoming animal" elaborated by Gilles Deleuze and Félix Guattari, who dismiss pets as commodified, oedipalized, and anthropomorphic projections of their owner's bourgeois individuality. Against such negative accounts of pets, the historian Keith Thomas argues that pets and their keepers had a crucial role in challenging dominant philosophical and scientific views concerning animal emotions and intelligence and thus the human monopoly on notions of personhood, thought, and subjectivity. Vicki Hearne and Donna Haraway have written more recently of the importance of pet–human relations as models for relating linguistically and empathically to otherness. I test such theories in a number of literary works and especially those of two exemplary modernist writers—Thomas Mann and Virginia Woolf, each of whom wrote a full-length novel or novella about dog–human relations—*Man and Dog* and *Flush*, respectively. Although dogs may thus appear to be typical of all pets in these chapters, my intent is not to generalize about them or about any species, but rather to insist, as do Mann and Woolf, on the singularity of each animal and of the relationships each demands. Such relationships can bring out the best and the worst of our capacities as human animals, and Mann and Woolf alike expose both the potential violence in our desires for pets and the potential for real love. It is in such relations, each author reveals, that the animals we live with—animals for whom sex and desire seems to operate without regard for gender— challenge our views of ourselves and bring us to question the processes of domestication we, too, undergo in order to become the gender and species we think we are. Mann and Woolf are especially significant in this regard, moreover, because, as I argue, their works engage with their contemporaries (primarily Friedrich Nietzsche in the case of Mann and Sigmund Freud in the case of Woolf) and thus with prominent theories regarding a human–animal divide and the alternatively threatening and heartening possibilities for breaching it.

Part III, "Grieving Animals," begins by taking up theorist Richard Klein's suggestion that "a dog should die like a dog" in order to ponder what a "proper death" might be for the creatures we love.[13] Here I begin by examining representations of human and animal death in *Flush* and in Leo Tolstoy's "story of a horse," "Strider," where the pomposity and extravagance of human rituals is contrasted with the ecological harmony of an unmarked animal death. I then move to consider what I see as a postmodernist and melancholic fascination with a kind of life in death or life feeding off death in Sam Taylor-Wood's short video piece *A Little Death* and Hélène Cixous's story "Shared at Dawn." Both works combine the incomplete mourning that Freud describes as melancholia with the exhilaration of Deleuze and Guattari's "becoming animal" such that boundaries of identity are lost in the representation of species' irreducible interdependence and mutual implication in each other's lives and deaths. Something is lost or dying, but we don't know what. In the end, however, what these modernist and postmodernist works share is a representation of animal death as unmourned, raising the question of the extent to which any animal may constitute what Judith Butler calls a "grievable life."[14]

This part and part IV bring together themes discussed in the previous sections—grief and death, shame and love, gender and species—in an effort to illustrate the difficulties we have in doing right by animals and in thinking ethically about what is our most common animal practice—killing them. Ethical thinking may itself be a contradictory endeavor when it comes to animals, if not a bêtise, because ethics itself grows out of a humanist and thus, if we believe Cary Wolfe, a necessarily anthropocentric tradition.[15] In chapter 7, "Thinking and Unthinking Animal Death," I begin with recent efforts by Derrida, Haraway, and Cora Diamond to problematize an ethics that is grounded in a "calculation" that questions how many it serves and how great is the cost or that is grounded in the belief that only humans know death. Although these writers represent different schools of thought, each argues that the ethical must grow instead out of an experience of shared mortality or bodily vulnerability that is, as Diamond writes, "painful to think." Such an ethics is derived from what she calls "the difficulty of reality"— a difficulty that our thinking often deflects in order to avoid the pain it can cause—both physically and psychically.[16] That our ways of knowing the world may constitute such a deflection of experience, especially the experience of death, is a problem that poet Rainer Maria Rilke raises in "The Eighth Elegy," written in 1922 and whose understanding of human thinking's dependence on language offers a counterpoint to Heidegger. Here, moreover, I argue for a theoretical link between animal studies and certain kinds of disability studies that has also emerged in conjunction with what has been called a "counterlinguistic turn" by focusing through two very different works on the experience of the death of an animal or, more accurately, the killing of an animal: Temple Grandin's autobiographical account of her autism, *Thinking in Pictures*, where she describes an act of kosher slaughter that is also something of an epiphany for her; and Coetzee's description of the euthanizing of an unwanted dog in *Disgrace*. In both of these scenes, a certain "technology" of death—by which I mean a very carefully executed form of killing, reveals what Agamben calls "bare life"—a zone of indeterminacy between human and animal as between human and machine. Language falters in that moment of such painful intensity that at it is depicted as sublime. But the sublimity of this posthumanist moment is also troubling, I suggest, because it privileges a spiritual or aesthetic ideal of love over love's prosaic manifestations.

It is with this notion of aestheticized killing in mind and in resistance to firm conclusions that I return to the ending of *Disgrace* and to David Lurie's decision to "give up" and euthanize the dog he has grown fond of. I read this act in light of what might first appear to be a very different account of our debt toward animals according to Rutgers law professor Gary Francione. Francione represents an extreme position in animal ethics and politics that can be described as authorizing the sacrifice of all domestic animals in the name of delivering humans from the crimes of sacrifice—crimes committed daily around the world. Lurie, I suggest, acts, however blindly, in the name of a similar "idea of the world"—a world freed of the animal eyes that remind us of our indignities and our shame. My critique of this ideal takes me to recent work in feminist ethics and "material feminism" and to what philosopher and animal trainer Vicki Hearne calls the "moral uprightnesses," if not the righteousness, that humans often assume in their dealings with other animals. In Hearne's writing, a philosophical and poetically inflected thinking about animals is combined with the practical knowledge that comes from the excitement and challenge of working with them as individuals. There is no moral high ground and no shame of shame. Indeed, if Hearne and the feminists I consider are indicative, the apparent blow that Charles Darwin struck to human pride seems to have had greater visible effects on a kind of masculine pride. This is true in Coetzee's novel as well: the life "we share with animals," as Lurie's daughter, Lucy, refers to it,[17] can make us feel small or powerless, deprive us of our place of privilege—a deprivation that is often associated with women and with which they have been familiar. What is to be found in that shared life is that we are not the only thinking beings or the autonomous authors of our history. Autonomy, because illusory, may be the "bête noir" of humanism and patriarchy alike.

In the end, this book returns to the heteronomy and heteroaffection of our lives as and with animals. To some extent, it is a queer ending that, like "queer ecology," celebrates the antiessentialism of evolution theory that "abolishes rigid boundaries between and within species" and assumes that we are related to all life forms.[18] However, if I argue that it would be wrong to essentialize the affinities between women and animals and thereby to reaffirm a gendered binary of nature and culture, so would I be cautious about an ecology that, according to Timothy Morton, advocates that all "strange strangers" must be brought into the collectivity, where the abolition of boundaries means there is no possibility for distinguishing the parasite from the host and where all "naturecultures" are accepted as a part of coevolution.[19] In a world where everything is considered part of a universal evolution, how can one distinguish ethical actions or responsibility? Would the recent BP-caused environmental disaster and the oil-coated animals in the Gulf of Mexico not then be just one more example of queer ecology?

Evolution may be antiteleological, as Darwin acknowledged, and that may mean there is no end in sight to what humans and other animals can yet become. Indeed, we are not and have never been the sole authors of a history that is always intertwined with the animals we feed and feed off of. But that is not a reason for us to shirk our human responsibility for the wrongs that our thinking has produced or for thinking in new ways about the humans we want to become. Thinking as and about animals is an art that requires rumination, as Nietzsche says about the art of reading in the book's epigraph; it should be haunted by our bêtises even as it takes stock of and pleasure in our capacities for rumination or for just walking (with) the dog.

THINKING ANIMALS

Part I

· ·

WHY
ANIMAL
STUDIES
NOW?

1

. . . .

A REPORT
ON THE ANIMAL TURN

Animal Studies and the Academy

It has been more than thirty years since Peter Singer introduced the term *speciesism* into philosophical parlance and wrote eloquently against a form of discrimination that went largely unnoticed both inside and outside academia. Although Singer has had enormous influence over the years in the area of animal rights, his effort to put the discrimination against nonhuman species on par with the prejudicial treatment and injustices caused by sexism or racism has had less success; the fight against speciesism has not had the same force in the academy, perhaps until now. In the past few years, there has been an explosion of conferences, books, and discussion networks around the question of the animal. On H-Net Animal, a lively and heated discussion took place around the question of whether "animal studies" is already or should become a new discipline and, if so, whether it should model itself on women's studies and ethnic studies.

Such questions are both pertinent and misconceived. Women's studies and ethnic studies programs demanded that the academy acknowledge and address the underrepresentation and misrepresentation groups of people under the forces of sexism and racism. This redress was to be done not only by focusing on those gaps and misrepresentations, but also and more importantly by bringing the voices of women and minorities into the academy to write and represent themselves. The result was that previously marginalized or silenced groups were no longer to be confined to the status of object but would be subjects of representations; their voices were speaking loudly and demanded to be heard. How can that situation be comparable to animal studies? True, for centuries nonhuman animals have been locked in representations authored by humans, representations that moreover have justified the use and abuse of nonhuman animals by humans. Unlike in women's studies or ethnic studies, however, those who constitute the objects of animal studies cannot speak for themselves, or at least they cannot speak any of the languages that the academy recognizes as necessary for such self-representation. Must they then be forever condemned to the status of objects?

Many of those who have taken nonhuman animals as their objects of study over the past ten or fifteen years (if we think back to the founding of the Great Ape Project in 1993) have nevertheless worked to prove that many animal species possess the basic capabilities deemed necessary for subjectivity: self-consciousness, rational agency, the capacity to learn and transmit language. Given a long tradition in Western philosophy that has declared the capacity for rational thought and its manifestation in language as that which distinguishes human from nonhuman animals, apes' proven ability to learn and teach sign language to other apes aims to show that a God-given human–animal divide is untenable and to confirm Darwin's apparently still controversial view that humans and apes are not so different. For Peter Singer and Paola Cavalieri, who founded the Great Ape Project, such findings are at the basis of efforts to include chimpanzees, gorillas, and orangutans in a "community of equals" with basic rights that must be protected by law.[1]

Alongside and sometimes against such attempts to bring (some) animals within the community of humans, an emerging facet of animal studies has increasingly questioned the justification for granting legal rights or protection to nonhuman animals on the grounds or to the extent that they are like humans. Influenced both by postmodern theory and by feminist and postcolonial critiques of the ways Western, educated Man has acted as the norm for what counts as human, recent discussions in animal studies have questioned to what extent our understanding of rights and protection are adequate for animals. Following feminists who have been critical of the way that the very notion of "women's rights" may reify a fictional identity of women as subordinate and thereby entrench women within their subordination, one might ask how the notion of "animal rights" might similarly entrench animals under a falsely unifying idea of "the animal"? The inequities of rights discourse, whether for humans or for animals, seems inevitable, and just as a prejudicial definition of the human has been used to grant privileges to some while excluding others, so the notion of animal rights privileges a particular group of animals— those who can demonstrate a capacity for so-called rational agency— and leaves others unprotected.[2] In this way, the question of the animal becomes an extension of those debates over identity and difference that have embroiled academic theory over the past quarter-century. If animal studies has come of age, it is perhaps because nonhuman animals have become a limit case for theories of difference, otherness, and power.

But how do we bring animal difference into theory? Can animals speak? And if so, can they be read or heard? Such questions have deliberate echoes of the title of Gayatri Spivak's seminal essay in postcolonial theory, "Can the Subaltern Speak?" where she warns that the critical establishment's attempt to give voice to dispossessed peoples will only result in those peoples' speaking the language of Western intellectuals or in their being further dependent on Western intellectuals to speak for them.[3] Her essay may serve as a warning to some who, for example, would try to teach apes to sign in order to have them tell humans what they want. Long before the existence of the Great Ape Project, this problem was exposed in Franz Kafka's 1919 story "A Report to an Academy." Red Peter, the story's narrator and protagonist, is presented as a representative of a minority or subaltern group: he is an ape. But the appropriateness of any of these designations is immediately brought into question as we learn that he is an ape-turned-human who has been singled out by the "academy" to give a report about his former life. Such a report, he admits, he is unable to give. His memory of his life as an ape has been erased as a result of his efforts to adopt his human captors' manners and language. Instead, he can only describe the process and progress of his assimilation from the moment of his capture to his current success as an artistic performer who smokes, drinks red wine, and converses like an "average European."[4]

Language is at the core of Kafka's critique of assimilation as a process that gives voice only by destroying the self that would speak. What is the self, Kafka's story asks, if it has no memory of its past and no means of representing it? Must that (animal) self be a blank page for others to write upon? Or might there be some other source of selfhood in his body, some physical locus where memory may be stored and known? Although "A Report to an Academy" is most often read as an allegory of German Jews in Prague, it illustrates the significance of a fundamental problematic of "the animal question": How does one have access to "the animal," whether it is the animal that must be "civilized" to exist in human society or the animals with whom we share the world? We might teach chimpanzees and gorillas to use sign language, but will that language enable them to speak of their animal lives or simply bring them to mimic (or ape) human values and viewpoints? Indeed, if they learn our language, will they still be animals?

Animal studies in this regard joins trauma studies both because of the violence done to animals and their habitats (what indeed has been called a genocide) and because of the difficulty of assessing how animals experience that violence.[5] Both raise questions about how one can give testimony to an experience that cannot be spoken or that may be distorted by speaking it. In Kafka's story, Red Peter has learned to live and, more important, to speak as a human, but with the result that he has lost the ability to remember his former life as an ape. Language gives him access to knowledge that he was an ape, but it does not allow him to represent that life. Indeed, his "report" takes the place of that former life that exists only as an aporia, a knowledge lost along with that of his ape life. He was wounded in his initial capture, and it is by virtue of his own self-flagellation that he is able to learn to speak. His speech is thus a kind of post-traumatic expression, symptomatic of, if not a repetition of that original wounding whose scars he readily displays even as he is unable to recall the events that led up to them.

Like trauma studies, animal studies thus stretches to the limit questions of language, epistemology, and ethics that have been raised in various ways by women's studies and postcolonial studies: how to understand and give voice to others or to experiences that seem impervious to our means of understanding; how to attend to difference without appropriating or distorting it; how to hear and acknowledge what it may not be possible to say. Here I want to trace the emergence of the "animal question" by focusing on three trends or moments in literary and critical theory for which the animal has become a test case: the linguistic turn, a counterlinguistic or affective turn, and the ethical turn. I will continue to make reference along the way to Kaka's story, much as J. M. Coetzee's feisty vegetarian protagonist Elizabeth Costello does in her lecture to an academic audience in *The Lives of Animals*.[6] I do so not because I feel like Red Peter, as Costello says she does, but because both she and Red Peter raise doubts about the academy's efficacy for dealing with this question.

Must Animals Mean What Humans Say?

In Lacanian psychoanalysis, subjectivity is born of a fall from wholeness into sexual division and desire and marked by a fall into language.[7] Language, as we see with Red Peter, irreparably splits the self between an experiential self and a speaking self who is never in the same place or time as the self that is to be represented. Although he is compelled to speak, his speech inevitably fails, becoming what might be read as a traumatic symptom. My point here is not to level traumas or to equate the trauma of coming to language with the trauma of physical injury or of Red Peter's wound. Rather, I wish to set up two different projects within animal studies that revolve around the question of language. On the one hand are those who look to our nonhuman others with envy or admiration precisely because they remain outside language and thus suggest the possibility of unmediated experience. On the other are those who would prove that animals do indeed speak and can tell us, however imperfectly, of their lives and their traumas.

"If a lion could speak, we could not understand him," Ludwig Wittgenstein wrote in a statement that, according to Cary Wolfe, might stand as epigraph to debates of the past century regarding animals, language, and subjectivity.[8] Wittgenstein's remark stands as an ambiguous retort to René Descartes, who, in his claim that speech marks a clear and infallible line of demarcation between humans and animals, warned, "Nor must we think, as did some of the ancients, that brutes talk although we do not understand their language."[9] To think so would be to attribute some form of rational thought and hence a soul to animals and thus ultimately to deny God. Since the late 1960s and early 1970s, however, research has proven both Descartes and Wittgenstein wrong (at least to the extent that lions may speak for animals in general) and affirmed (though not without contestation) that, indeed, some animals can be taught to use language and can be understood. Washoe, a chimpanzee, was just the first of the great apes to be taught sign language and demonstrate that he could even combine signs in new and even metaphorical ways. The research that Roger Fouts began with Washoe and Loulis was continued by Sue Savage-Rumbaugh and the bonobos, Kanzi and Panbanisha, at the Great Ape Trust in Iowa.[10] Against the skepticism of linguists and scientists who said it was impossible, Savage-Rumbaugh showed that Kanzi and Panbanisha could indeed learn to use and to respond to full sentences and understand the demands of grammar as well as of signs. Moreover, she discovered, they would say more when they had something to say and thus were not merely imitating. Kanzi used the keyboard more than three hundred times the day he was separated from his mother, from which Savage-Rumbaugh concluded: "What I had to do is come up with an environment . . . a world that would foster the acquisition of these lexical symbols in Kanzi and a greater understanding of spoken human language."[11]

Savage-Rumbaugh's research seemed to prove that these apes were not simply "reacting" to stimuli in the Cartesian sense in which animals can obey a fixed behavior, but "responding" to humans and to each other with an awareness of language and the world around them.[12] Moreover, her research also raised new questions as to the relation between language and world and how one might affect rather than simply translate the other. In other words, her research made it imperative to ask whether language allowed Kanzi to express his thoughts or whether it replaced those thoughts with available and communicable signs. "He asked her for food. He asked her for affection. He asked her for help finding his mom."[13]

Similar questions about language are raised by Irene Pepperberg's research on her African Grey parrot, Alex. In her view, the linguistic deficiencies attributed to the parrot were more correctly deficiencies on the part of the researchers, who hadn't figured out how to give him a reason to speak. "People used to think birds weren't intelligent," said Pepperberg; "well they used to think women weren't intelligent either."[14] Much like Savage-Rumbaugh, Pepperberg saw language not as the putting together of sign and signified, but as a response to a social environment in which one is motivated to communicate either by imitating models or by challenging rivals for food, affection, and attention. Alex's last words to Pepperberg before he died were "I love you," a simple phrase whose meaning has been as debated as much as Alex's ability to understand it. Were these words an indication of cognitive ability (response) or merely reactive imitation? But the question, as Verlyn Klinkenborg made clear in a *New York Times* editorial, is not a question for animals alone. "To wonder what Alex recognized when he recognized words is also to wonder what humans recognize when we recognize words."[15] It is to wonder how recognition and response (or intention) are ever clearly distinct from imitation. When it comes to language, are not all of us dependent on a field of signification that precedes us, making it difficult to say that language itself is ever not imitative? How do we know what our lovers mean when they say "I love you"?

The alternative to language as imitation entails its own absurdities, as Wolfe suggests in recalling Wittgenstein. "What can it mean to imagine a language we cannot understand, spoken by a being who cannot speak?"[16] The emphasis must be on our own impoverished capacities, Vicki Hearne reminds us, because Wittgenstein did not say that the lion could not speak, only that we could not understand him. A poet, philosopher, and animal trainer, Hearne adds, moreover, that Wittgenstein's statement, like Descartes's, has been used to evade the fundamental "tragedy of language," a notion that she takes from Stanley Cavell. We experience this tragedy when we acknowledge that there is another consciousness there, a consciousness we desperately desire to know through language, but that may remain impenetrable. Training, for Hearne, is a means to begin to penetrate that consciousness, but only to the extent that we humans can relinquish the stance of impenetrability that we claim for ourselves and with which we protect ourselves from being known by the animals we live with.

Hearne writes about animal training in a Cavellean mode, a mode that is full of tragedy as well as comedy and that is fundamentally about language and "what it can be." Language, in her view, is not a matter of attaching a sign to a signified. "If we describe the integrity of a language as the physical, intellectual and spiritual distance talking enables the speakers of that language to travel together, then it looks very much as though the dog and the horse have a greater command of language than chimpanzees do."[17] In other words, through training, dogs and horses are given tools for entering a relationship within which they can be said to speak, not merely to react. We may not always understand them, but it is imperative that we acknowledge that they may have things to say. Hearne gives the example of teaching dogs to track or follow a scent. Once they learn their job, they become much better at it than we humans could ever be because we can't read or even find the scents that exist as signs for them and that they read. There is no question of imitation.

"What is linguistic in this relation?" asks Paul Patton of the training of horses. Despite Hearne's insistence that training is a form of communication that depends on dogs' and horses' capacities for language, Patton, a professor of philosophy and a dressage rider, raises concerns about the coercive measures of training. "Both training and riding involve the exercise of power over the animal and, contrary to the view of many philosophers and trainers, relations of communication are not external but immanent to relations of power."[18] What this means is not that power lies only on one side or the other of the relationship, but rather that horses and humans alike are subservient to patterns of semiosis that precede them—whether those signs be linguistic or somatic; whether they consist in words or in touch, pressure, and tone. Teaching dogs to track and training horses in dressage involve communication between beings who are "unequally endowed with capacities for language, for hearing and scent discrimination, or for movement and kinesthetic sensation. As a consequence, human–animal relations cannot be regarded as incomplete versions of human–human relations but must be regarded as complete versions of relations between different kinds of animals," says Patton.[19] In such relations, the problem of language is less one of imitation than of translation.

Perhaps what is linguistic in training is that relations between different kinds of animals are like relations between humans. Training, like language, compels me to acknowledge that there is another phenomenal world, or *Umwelt* (as ethologist Jakob von Uexküll called it),[20] even as it reveals that our worlds (and our means of expressing them) are not commensurate. Training cannot give me your world or give you mine—although it may allow us to find a place of intersection between our worlds. Hearne's writing on training illuminates the problem of skepticism that has been central to the linguistic turn and takes the discussion of this problem a step farther. For her, training necessitates skepticism regarding our knowledge of the other and, through this, our knowledge of the world. It also sheds light on the Cavellean skepticism that concerns what others (myself included) can know of me. Hearne writes that horses stand as a rebuke to our knowledge because they seem to know us better than we can ever know them. Cavell comments on this notion in an exchange with Hearne where he writes that the horse "is a rebuke to our unreadiness to be understood . . . our will to remain obscure."[21] Here, skepticism is revealed as a kind of crutch, a protection against that which may be unmediated and which we may fear as much as we disbelieve it is possible. We may know animals in ways they cannot—we may know their breeds, their color, their weight, their names, their "histories"—but they may also know us in ways that we cannot know because they know the world and us by other means. Thus, Hearne agrees with Cavell that when it comes to dogs or horses (or perhaps chimpanzees and parrots), the issue is not that we are too skeptical (of their cognitive abilities, for instance), but that we are not skeptical enough of our skepticism and why we embrace it.

Ineffable Animality and the Counterlinguistic Turn

If the linguistic turn insisted that there we have no access to unmediated experience or knowledge, but only to representations that are themselves fraught with linguistic and ideological baggage, the turn to animals can be seen as responding to a desire for a way out of this "prison-house of language."[22] It responds to a desire to know that there are beings or objects with ways of knowing and being that resist our flawed systems of language and who may know us and themselves in ways we can never discern.

The difficulty, of course, is discovering how and where to cite what is outside of our language, if, indeed, we have access to that outside. Post-structuralism insisted that we humans can never get outside of our linguistic frameworks and that we have no knowledge and no experience that escapes language. In this regard, the turn to animals may be seen as an attempt not only to escape from post-structuralism's linguistic trap but to reexamine its confines. Animals are at the very origin of our systems of representation. According to John Berger, animals like those drawn on the caves of Lascaux seventeen thousand years ago were our very first symbols.[23] But insofar as language and the possibility for self-representation constitute that by which humans have distinguished themselves from nonhuman animals, we must ask whether our representations act to bridge or to increase the distance between us and them, if not between us and the animals we are.[24] In *The Postmodern Animal*, Steve Baker writes that there was no modern or modernist animal because pictures had to be about the act of picturing before they were anything else. "The animal is the first thing to be ruled out of modernism's bounds."[25] In other words, modernism's insistence that representation can refer only to itself or to its specific linguistic or ideological system and modernism's consequent privileging of the act and method of representation over and above the represented object rule out ever getting to the animal as animal. Modernism thus can be seen as a precursor to post-structuralism's representational cage.

Such ruling out of the animal is also at the crux of Kafka's "A Report to an Academy." The story can be read as an allegory of our entry into modernity through enlightenment and the concomitant loss of animality, a loss that has regrettable results. This is one reason that Red Peter is quick to dissociate his liberation from his ape cage with freedom. "I fear that perhaps you do not quite understand what I mean by 'way out.' I use the expression in its fullest and most popular sense. I deliberately do not use the word 'freedom'" (198). In "What

Is Enlightenment?" Michel Foucault points out that the term *way out* or *Ausgang* is the one Immanuel Kant uses to define enlightenment (*Aufklärung*) as a negation or difference.[26] Kant understands enlightenment as the process by which humans will escape from their former subjection to despotic rule or irrational authority and find their rightful status as autonomous subjects. The state of subjection, in other words, is comparable to the status of animals or infants who must rely on others to make rational choices for them. For Kafka's Red Peter, however, escape from the state of animal is not to be regarded as the achievement of freedom or autonomy. Even as Red Peter describes his transformation as a "gradual enlightenment," the phrase indicates an alternative to the cage as a means of coercion and an imposed conformity to the "way of humanity." "And so I learned things, gentlemen. Ah, one learns when one has to; one learns when one needs a way out; one learns at all costs. One stands over oneself with a whip, one flays oneself at the slightest opposition. My ape nature fled out of me, head over heels and away" (203). Condemned to be free as a human, Red Peter learns how to beat his ape self into obedience.

Kafka's story poses the question, "At what cost enlightenment?" To the extent that the Enlightenment has, as Foucault suggests, "determined, at least in part, what we are, what we think, and what we do today,"[27] must we not also wonder what it deterred us from thinking, what it made us leave behind or whip into submission? The turn to animals in art as in theory is to attempt to envision a different understanding of what we humans are and consequently to enlarge or change the possibilities for what we can think and what we can do in the world. The postmodern turn to animals that Baker explores in his book is part of this ongoing reassessment of Enlightenment ideals and a concurrent effort to give new definition to the human not as a being opposed to animals, but as animal. The project is similar to the literary and historical focus on the body over the past few decades—whether the body is understood as the inseparable support and interface of thought and language or as the material register or trace of experiences lived outside of or prior to language and interpretation, much like Red Peter's wound. How to recuperate those experiences that may have been forgotten or repudiated has been the focus of recent historical writings concerned with traumatic events. In

The Open: Man and Animal, Giorgio Agamben takes the phrase "the open wound that is my life" from Georges Bataille as a metaphor for the existential trauma of life caught in the caesura between human and animal, "the central emptiness, the hiatus that—within man— separates man and animal."²⁸ Inferring that efforts to articulate or locate that emptiness can result only in violence, Agamben asks that we "let it be" outside knowledge and "outside being." In *Sublime Historical Experience,* Dutch historian F. R. Ankersmit similarly brings notions of trauma and the sublime together by virtue of their disruption of normal ways of understanding the world and our selves. To focus on the sublime is to recognize the dangerous inadequacy of our language for communicating experiences outside our consciousness, much as Red Peter realized that any human representation of his life as an ape would necessarily be a "misrepresentation." But even though Red Peter has forgotten his former life and is unable to represent it, that life must still be considered a part of who he is. "We are not only the past we (can) remember (as the historists [*sic*] have always argued)," writes Ankersmit, "but *also* the past we can *forget.*"²⁹ The attention to the sublime, as Martin Jay describes it, is an attempt to access that lost or repressed experience that is outside of or prior to language and that may bring us to a "deeper reality."³⁰

The privileging of a "sublime" disruption or disassociation of normal ways of knowing is central also to the writings of Gilles Deleuze and Félix Guattari, which have inspired a postmodern if not posthuman project in animal studies. Their notion of "becoming animal," which they elaborate in *A Thousand Plateaus: Capitalism and Schizophrenia,* is an attempt to undo accepted and recognizable definitions of the human by replacing notions of exterior form and function with notions of affects and intensities and flows of movement as means to describe and value life. Their notion of experience as a tactile or visceral affair exceeds the possibilities of language to contain or identify it because becoming "produces nothing but itself."³¹ There is no identity or subject that precedes becoming and no identity that a subject becomes. Hence, one cannot even be said to become *an* animal; one becomes "becoming." Becoming animal is a creative rather than intellectual endeavor, and Deleuze and Guattari associate it with the writing or artistic process. "Either stop writing or write like a rat," they assert.[32] Write like a rat? The point is that this writing cannot be done through imitation. The term *like* in this phrase demands at once the undoing of our assumptions of rat identity and a creative inhabiting of a rat's body, for this is the purpose of Art. The artist must be responsible to the ever-changing intensities of speeds and matter that is the life of a body.

It should come as no surprise that the author Deleuze and Guattari most associate with "becoming animal" is Kafka. They describe Kafka's writing itself as a form of becoming where words are wrenched or uprooted from their meanings and turned into "deterritorialized sounds." Thus, in reference to Kafka's *Metamorphosis* they write:

> Kafka deliberately kills all metaphor, all symbolism, all significa-
> tion, no less than all designation. Metamorphosis is the contrary of
> metaphor. There is no longer any proper sense or figurative sense,
> but only a distribution of states that is part of the range of the
> word. The thing and other things are no longer anything but inten-
> sities overrun by deterritorialized sound. . . . It is no longer a ques-
> tion of a resemblance between the comportment of an animal and
> that of a man. . . . The animal does not speak "like" a man but pulls
> from the language tonalities totally lacking in signification. . . . To
> make the sequences vibrate, to open the word onto unexpected
> internal intensities—in short, an asignifying *intensive utilization*
> of language.[33]

Such privileging of becoming and the sublime are part of what can be called a "counterlinguistic turn," an effort either to lay claim to what lies outside language or to destroy language and the meaning-ful relations it enables.[34] In contrast to Hearne's attempts to found a community of humans and animals through the meaningful rela-tions that language makes possible, Deleuze and Guattari want to free humans and animals from meaning altogether and thus to undo the very identities that confirm a distinction between human and ani-mal. For them, Kafka's animals are unidentifiable creatures who effect upheavals of the human self, turning it into something it was not and could not conceive of. Indeed, in a theoretical move familiar to stu-dents of deconstruction, differences between animals and humans are displaced onto differences within the human: to deterritorialize is to become aware of the animal otherness within the human.

Animals and the Ethical Turn

With Agamben, as with Deleuze and Guattari, theory's concern for the animal moved quite a distance from questions of rights or even protection for animals. In both, we find an attempt to locate what might be called a "postmodern sublime" in extreme experience that risks an aestheticization of trauma or, at the least, a denial of its effects on the flesh. Thus, what Deleuze and Guattari see as a liberatory plunge into animal difference, outside the confines of human signification and into a state of animality (like that of Gregor Samsa in Kafka's *The Metamorphosis*), has, indeed, little to say about the actual animals we live with. Donna Haraway's recent assessment is more than telling in this respect. Referring especially to Deleuze and Guattari's dismissal of domestic animals as figuring into ideas of becoming, she writes, "I am not sure I can find in philosophy a clearer display of misogyny, fear of aging, incuriosity about animals, and horror at the ordinariness of flesh, here covered by the alibi of an anti-Oedipal and anticapitalist project."[35] In a related vein, Dominick LaCapra warns against Agamben's evasive fascination with a sublime abyss. Noting that Agamben "does not thematize the relation of his thought to trauma," LaCapra does it for him: "One could redescribe Agamben's 'central emptiness' as an insufficiently situated version of transhistorical, structural, or existential trauma that, in Agamben's account, may well induce an evasion or misconstruction of specific historical, social and political problems, including the status and use of the animal in society."[36]

It is in part in reaction to such theories' inability to deal with the concerns of live animals (including aging women) that animal studies is coming of age in conjunction with theory's ethical turn. Animals are and should be of concern not only as instruments of theory, not only because they affect us, but because our lives also affect them. Ethics in this respect is not a concern for "the good." We can no longer say with certainty what the good is. Nor does ethics refer only to a Foucauldian ethos or care of the self, although a mastery of the animal self or body is relevant. Rather, the ethical turn that has followed in the wake of deconstruction is an attempt to recognize and extend care to others while acknowledging that we may not know what the best form of care is for an other whom we cannot presume to know. It is a concern with and for alterity, especially insofar as alterity brings us to the limits of our own self-certainty and certainty about the world. This is an area that has brought animal and trauma studies together: we can recognize the serious harms rendered to victims of horrific acts, but we cannot count on those victims to tell us their stories or what to do about them.

Deconstruction has revealed the unstable foundations and false oppositions to "the animal" on which notions of the human have been built. But it has also made it difficult, if not impossible, to proceed from acts of representation to acts of engagement with others who are or have been oppressed in some way. Recent efforts to speak about that which is supposedly outside language and outside the discursive systems that determine experience as much as they may reflect it show that animal studies has turned away from deconstruction's insistence that there is no *hors texte*. Some writers in the field, furthermore, would claim that this effort to attend to the ineffable is itself an ethical act. The dilemma is a familiar one to feminist theorists who in the past, faced with their own pronouncements that language is not only unstable but also patriarchal (and thus foreign to the expression of women's desires), nevertheless encouraged forms of writing that would point toward or imagine an "elsewhere" outside of language. Such a practice was associated with a practice of hearing otherwise and with a nonmastery of knowledge that was understood to be expressly ethical.[37] For some theorists of trauma, the opacity of traumatic events to representation is similarly regarded as engendering new forms of testimonial or, in Cathy Caruth's terms, the "imperative of a speaking that awakens others."[38] Kelly Oliver writes of the act of witnessing as foundational to the experience of responsible subjectivity because witnessing engages "the sense of agency and responseability that are constituted in the infinite encounter with otherness, which is fundamentally ethical."[39]

Attempts to articulate a posthuman (or posthumanist) ethics— ethics toward an unknowable or "incalculable" other—have more recently made it imperative that we look beyond the Kantian foundations of the ethical in a human subject. The term *posthuman* first appeared in relation to the realm of informatics, where the "thinking life" is shared by humans and machines alike. As Katherine Hayles uses the term in her book *How We Became Posthuman*,[40] the word *posthuman* refers to a conglomerate of independent agents of information that can flow easily between human and machine. The very notion of artificial intelligence thus challenged the enlightenment view of the human as sole proprietor of consciousness and agency. Such dismantling of the enlightenment "human" furthermore offered a new path for feminists such as Donna Haraway, who invoked the "cyborg" as a means of creating alliances between feminism and technology and of contesting entrenched dualisms of nature and culture that had been obstacles to imagining new, postmodernist, and perhaps posthumanist identities.

But what was also explicit in Haraway's "Manifesto for Cyborgs,"[41] if underemphasized, was the simultaneous critique of the boundary between human and animal and hence of the belief in human exceptionalism that this boundary maintained. Just as Haraway moved her focus from cyborgs to dogs, so animal studies more generally has brought attention to a notion of the posthuman that acknowledges human animals as having coevolved with innumerable species without whom we would not be who we are and with whom we share our environment and its resources. Barbara Herrnstein-Smith writes:

> As "posthumanists," we have begun to chart the costs and limits of the classic effort to maintain an essential species barrier and have sought to diminish those costs and to press against those limits in our own conceptual and other practices. The *telos*—aim or endpoint—of these developments is conceived here, however, not as the universal recognition of a single, comprehensive order of Nature or Being but, rather, as an increasingly rich and operative appreciation of our irreducibly multiple and variable, complexly valenced, infinitely reconfigurable relations with other animals, including each other.[42]

Animals, of course, have long been a focus of Haraway's work, but it is only recently that she has turned from examining how the language of otherness has structured scientific research on animals to questioning what we can learn from our actual engagements *with* animals. Dogs are not "surrogates for theory," Haraway insists; "they are not here just to think with. They are here to live with."[43] And it is through both research of their evolutionary complexity and deep attention to their embodied capacities that Haraway seeks a model for relating to "significant otherness."[44] Such "ethical relating," as she calls it, once again is said to demand a relation to what cannot be known or at least known in advance—their needs and capacities are not ours, even as they respond to ours.

In its focus on values of love or respect or achievement, Haraway's language of training, like Vicki Hearne's, has been criticized as overly anthropomorphic and anything but posthuman. But the turn to ethics in animal studies has brought a new focus on the notion of anthropomorphism, regarded not only as a problem, but also as a potentially productive, critical tool that has similarities to empathy within recent historical research. That anthropomorphism may have its place for rethinking human difference is the motivating idea in Lorraine Daston and Gregg Mitman's collected volume *Thinking with Animals: New Perspectives on Anthropomorphism.* "Before either animal individuality or subjectivity can be imagined, an animal must be singled out as a promising prospect for anthropomorphism," Daston and Mitman write in their introduction; the animal must be seen as capable of pain and pleasure, as having his or her own affects and capacities.[45] On the one hand, as a process of identification, the urge to anthropomorphize the experience of another, like the urge to empathize with that experience, risks becoming a form of narcissistic projection that erases boundaries of difference. On the other hand, as a feat of attention to another and of imagination regarding the other's perspective, this urge is what brings many of us to act on behalf of the perceived needs and desires of an other/animal.[46] Coetzee's Elizabeth Costello calls this urge "sympathy," but she means the same thing: it is the faculty that some poets have that "allows us to share at times the being of another."[47]

The term *critical empathy*, which has arisen in trauma theory (and especially trauma related to the Holocaust), is relevant here. In her book *Empathic Vision*, Jill Bennett distinguishes critical empathy from

the "crude" empathy that Bertolt Brecht critiqued as overidentifica-
tion. Critical empathy is a "conjunction of affect and critical awareness [that] may be understood to constitute the basis of an empathy
grounded not in affinity (*feeling for* another insofar as we can imagine
being that other) but on a *feeling for* another that entails an encounter
with something irreducible and different, often inaccessible."[48] With
this in mind, we might then want to call an ethical relating to animals (whether in theory or in art) "critical anthropomorphism" in the
sense that we open ourselves to touch and to be touched by others
as fellow subjects and may imagine their pain, pleasure, and need in
anthropomorphic terms, but stop short of believing that we can know
their experience. In addition, critical anthropomorphism must begin
with the acknowledgment that the irreducible difference that animals
may represent for us is one that is also within us and within the term
human. Which human are we allegedly projecting onto animals?[49]
When is anthropomorphism another form of zoomorphism?

The dangers of essentializing notions of "the animal" and of "the
human" through those notions are most emphatically addressed in
the last essays Jacques Derrida wrote before his death. In *The Animal
That Therefore I Am*, he denounces the phrase *the animal* as a "catch-
all concept" used to "designate every living thing that is held not to be
human."[50] Animals have been homogenized into a singular concept,
he argues, through blindness to the differences that exist among animals as among humans. The question of "the animal" is a blind spot
in philosophy, an unquestioned foundation upon which the notion
of the human has been constructed. Writing against this tradition,
Derrida writes of both the shame and the vulnerability he feels when
looked at naked by his cat. "It has its point of view regarding me," he
writes. "The point of view of the absolute other, and nothing will have
ever done more to make me think through this absolute alterity of
the neighbor than the moments when I see myself naked under the
gaze of a cat."[51] Derrida thus suggests that the struggle for recognition
that from G. W. F. Hegel through Jean-Paul Sartre is described as a
struggle between men might find its ultimate expression between a
human and an (other) animal. Describing the other with the Levinas-
sian term *neighbor*, moreover, he qualifies that confrontation less as
an adversarial struggle than as an ethical one—an attempt to relate

across unknowable distance. Thinking itself, Derrida says, begins in such moments when we see an animal look at us, see ourselves placed in the context of an other world, where living, speaking, dying, being mean otherwise.

"The animal looks at us, and we are naked before it. Thinking perhaps begins there," Derrida writes.[52] Thinking begins in the space between the animal I am and am not—a space that is also at the foundation of thinking the ethical. Our very notion of ethical relating has been grounded in a humanism that gives permission to act unethically toward animals—sacrificing them as food, clothing, medicine. This is the ethical founded in a (often unacknowledged) notion of the human defined by its capacities: thought, reason, agency. And yet the notion of "what is proper to man"—whether it be language or consciousness or agency—has been and will continue to be shown as an illusory exclusivity, either because shared by some animals or not possessed by some humans. That is why Derrida shifts his attention from our capacities, whether in a Cartesian sense as language and reason or in a Deleuzean sense as affects and intensities, to focus on our shared vulnerabilities, our inabilities (*impouvoirs*). For a posthumanist ethics, Derrida elsewhere returns to Jeremy Bentham's question: "it is not whether they can reason, but whether they suffer." From this vantage point, the "industrial, scientific and technical violence" that is wrought upon nonhuman animals must change. "The relations between humans and animals *must* change."[53]

Echoing Derrida, Wolfe writes, "there can be no science of ethics, no 'calculation' of the subject whose ethical conduct is determined in a linear way by scientific discoveries about animals (or anything else)." Wolfe critiques the scientific but essentially humanist underpinnings of certain animal rights philosophy (such as the Great Ape Project) that would recognize the moral status of certain animals "not because of their wonder and uniqueness, not because of their difference, but because they are inferior versions of ourselves."[54] Posthumanist ethical relations, for Wolfe as for Derrida, cannot be grounded on rational principles or scientific measures of brain activity or capacity for language. In the domain of ethics, such normative rules, if not incompatible with alterity, end up by privileging the alterity of the human and defining the human in ways that exclude some humans.

Even as Wolfe deftly points out the stubborn humanism at the base of most efforts to extend ethical concepts to animals, he also senses a necessary double bind—the need to advocate certain principles of rights or protection with the knowledge of that faulty foundation. The only way to move beyond what might be called this "strategic ethics" (recalling feminism's strategic essentialism) is not through any form of "becoming animal," but on the contrary through an engagement with others through theory. Theory may reveal ethics as an essentially human duty, but only by constantly challenging our understanding of what it is to be human. "My premise," says Wolfe, "has been that maintaining a commitment to distinctly posthumanist ways of theorizing the questions at hand . . . will enhance our understanding of the embeddedness and entanglement of the 'human' in all that it is not, in all that used to be thought of as its opposites or its others."[55]

This entanglement of human and nonhuman is what Derrida exposes in looking at his cat. It is not a denial of difference by any means, but rather an attention to the construction of difference at the very foundation of the ethical. And this is true for the ethical difference itself. The ethical, like the animal, is a category of the human. Indeed, it is in the name of the human as an ethical animal and because of what the violence done to "the animal" does to the image of humanity that, Derrida says, change will come. Ethics, for Derrida as for Kant and Emmanuel Levinas—perhaps the thinker most important for Derrida's ethical thinking—is and remains one of the dividing lines between humans and animals. An animal *can* address us. But until a sense of disinterested obligation can be witnessed in and by animals, Derrida is not ready to relinquish an ethical decision as a human duty or to shift the ethical difference to the animal realm, for doing so would be to run the risk of the worst forms of biologism. "What I am saying is that we must not invoke the violence among animals, in the jungle or elsewhere, as a pretext for giving ourselves over to the worst forms of violence."[56] The ethical imperative, then, for Derrida as for Haraway and Wolfe, is analysis of the very construction of the ethical, especially because ethics is used to configure the human as well as its animal other. We must always be vigilant of the ways our promotion of an ethical treatment of animals can and has been used to discriminate among groups of humans as well as of how ethical treatment of humans is often performed at the expense of animals. But there can be no law of ethics. What is ethical depends on situated contexts and knowledge. To be ethical is to weigh incompatible needs and inevitable sufferings and to come to a "least bad solution."[57] Indeed, for Derrida, to be ethical is to take the risk of deciding the undecidable: "The difficulty of ethical responsibility is that the response cannot be formulated as a 'yes or no'; that would be too simple. It is necessary to give a singular response, within a given context, and to take the risk of a decision by enduring the undecidable. In every case, there are two contradictory imperatives."[58]

Why animal studies now? It has become clear that the idea of "the animal"—the instinctive being with presumably no access to language, texts, or abstract thinking—has functioned as an unexamined foundation on which the idea of the human and hence the humanities have been built. It has also become clear, primarily through advances in a range of scientific studies of animal language, culture, and morality, that this exclusion has taken place on false grounds. As our improved understanding of animal lives and cultures changes, so must we change our view of the nature of the human and of the humanities. Thought, consciousness, and language are not humans' exclusive property. Indeed, there is no shared consensus on what these properties consist in. From the perspective of theory, animal studies may have emerged only in time for its existence to be outdated. Much like the "women" in women's studies, the "animal" in animal studies must be placed under erasure.[59]

And yet even as the humanities may, as Cary Wolfe suggests, be struggling to catch up with this "radical revalution of non-human animals,"[60] recent theoretical reflections on the question of the animal suggest that scientific research cannot offer sufficient grounds on which to construct a postwomen, a postanimal, or a posthuman ethics. Perhaps in contrast to the sciences, much of contemporary theory gives value precisely to the ways animals resist our tools of analysis even as they succumb to our invasive and dominating need to know. "The animal question" has thus replaced the "woman question" (indeed, it is easier for many to contemplate animals as significant others than women) in coming to stand for what is incalculable—it points to an aporia in our reason and our knowledge—but also unavoidable in and for our lives.

"I am not appealing for any man's verdict," Red Peter says at the end of Kafka's story, "I am only imparting knowledge, I am only making a report" (204). Speaking from a place of uncertainty, a place that is neither wholly ape nor wholly human, Red Peter figures the space of theoretical investigation today. It is a space of productive inquiry but offers no clear standard of how to measure progress. "Do not tell me that it was not worth the trouble," Red Peter says, realizing that the fate he escaped still claims the lives of others. He admits that he "cannot bear to see" the half-trained female chimpanzee who is brought to him for "comfort" in the evening, "for she has the insane look of the bewildered half-broken animal in her eye" (204). Looking at her, he sees the distance he has traveled, but he also recognizes her suffering—something "no one else sees." Red Peter cannot deny the existence of animal suffering, but neither has he gained clear criteria for doing something about it. More critically, it would appear that his professional success, like his virility and indeed his humanity, depend on not acting upon that recognition and thus refusing kinship with the chimpanzee.[61]

In the wake of post-structuralist and postmodern decenterings that have displaced the human as a standard for knowledge, theory finds itself in a similar predicament. It cannot avoid seeing the animal suffering around us, but it has contradictory foundations on which to judge the good or the right thing to do about it. Responding to an urgent call for concern, those of us working on "the animal question" may only be able, like Red Peter, to make a report, but such reports, it is to be hoped, will enable us to make decisions (for that is our human prerogative and responsibility) that will, to the best of our imperfect and partial knowledge, enhance the lives of all animals, ourselves included.

2

· · · · · · · · · · · · · · · · · · · ·

SEEING ANIMALS

(In)Visible Animality

In chapter 1, I addressed some of the similarities and differences between animal studies today and women's studies when the latter emerged as an academic field in the 1970s. The comparison between these fields (as well as minority and ethnic studies) is especially revealing when we turn to the matter of visibility and visual representations. In the early days of women's studies, as of ethnic studies, there was a pronounced drive to make women and minorities visible as participants, authors, and makers of culture rather than mere consumers or enablers. This task was to be done not only by focusing on misrepresentations, but also, more important, by bringing women's and minorities' voices into the academy to write and represent themselves. Previously marginalized or silenced, these groups were no longer to be confined to the status of object but rather were to be subjects or authors of their own representations; their voices were speaking loudly and demanded to be heard.

The situation with animal studies is somewhat similar, but there are clearly important differences. Animals, too, have been either invisible or locked in representations authored by humans, representations that moreover have justified their use and abuse by humans. Indeed, their invisibility has been of an equally insidious kind for us—the invisibility of factory farms and of the experimentation and abuse that chimps have suffered. One scientist's response to the 2001 birth of the first genetically modified primate was: "We're at an extraordinary moment in the history of humans."[1] But what about in the history of chimpanzees? Do they not have a history? Well, not in the sense that Hegel gave to that term. Nietzsche, too, wrote that animals live "unhistorically," knowing neither "the meaning of yesterday or today."[2] Nietzsche would, however, regard this lack of knowledge as a gift.

Although such historical invisibility must certainly contribute to the status of nonhuman animals as expendable objects, how to bring them into a visibility that might rescue them from a horrific fate is less than clear. And this problem is, for better or for worse, a dilemma for us humans because even though artwork by chimps or elephants has produced much cash for some dealers lately, we cannot expect to find a chimp authoring his or her own self-representation—at least not in the languages we recognize.

The question then becomes what sort of visibility we are trying to create. Or the question may be whether it is possible to render nonhuman animals visible without fixing their meanings. With regard to the issues over the representation of women, it became clear that promoting any particular image of woman, even a so-called positive image, could be counterproductive—counter to essentializing tendencies that would confine women into a preconceived mold or function. In a similar fashion, the representation of various nonhuman animals poses the question of how they might be seen on their own terms rather than seen as fitting into categories imposed upon them by humans. This is a question of ontology and aesthetics, if not of ethics—and there may be times when the demands of one realm may be at odds with the demands of another. From an aesthetic perspective, one might condemn sentimentality—something the representation of animals has often been associated with. From another angle, there is only so much torture or suffering that humans are willing or perhaps able to see and pay attention to. Representations of torture or suffering may thus in a contradictory way be another way of allowing us not to see the animal—to look away.

Do we in fact see "the animal" rather than an animal? *The animal* is a term that Derrida has reminded us not to use: "*Animal* is a word that men have given themselves the right to give. . . . They have given themselves the word in order to corral a large number of living beings within a single concept."[3] The question of animals' ontology is a blind spot in philosophy, even as, Derrida shows, it is a question on which the ontology of Man has been constructed. Not unlike the term *woman* or *slave*, *animal* is a term that men have given others so as to name themselves the agents of history, freedom, thought. But are animals only lacking? Is their nature or "being" only an impoverished form of human "being"? Clearly not, and the issue becomes how to see and represent their being outside our terms of reference and without claiming an essentialized otherness. To put the term *animal* under scrutiny is to accept that the differences between animals may be far greater than what we all share and that we may be more like some animals than they are like each other. It is also to acknowledge that there may be something of "the animal" that we long to know and represent, if only because we believe (or perhaps deny) that we share that something with them.

Here I first address the difficulties of thinking "that something," which is to say, of thinking animal being, before I turn to two very different artists who have attempted to represent animals' being.

Philosophical Ruminations on Animal Being

What is an animal's being? The question has inspired a great deal of skepticism and a great deal of faith in recent years: skepticism about what we can actually know of nonhuman animals and their worlds; faith that they do indeed have worlds, that they are subjects of their worlds despite our lack of certainty about them. Skepticism regarding animals, of course, is not new. What is significant, perhaps, is a growing acceptance that skepticism must not deter us from believing what we cannot know with certainty to be true and that we need not doubt the existence of what we cannot prove. Skepticism, in other words, has turned from animals to the power of reflection itself and hence toward the distinguishing mark of the so-called superiority of the so-called rational animal. In *The Animal That Therefore I Am*, Derrida insists that the wars being raged over animal life are wars also

· · · · · · · · · · ·

about "what we call 'thinking.'" And he adds, "The animal looks at us, and we are naked before it. Thinking perhaps begins there."[4] To consider that animals look and look at us is to imagine that animals think (about us), which changes what it means to be human: thought can no longer be regarded as our exclusive and defining privilege. It also, we shall see, changes what we understand to be thought. To think about animals or to think about animals thinking necessitates a change in our understanding of thought. And it is at this site of thinking otherwise, this site where thinking is turned back on itself to become undone or unthought, that animal being—human or nonhuman—is said to emerge.

Can the very act of thinking be regarded as an impediment for understanding the being of animals? Thomas Nagel's much cited 1974 essay "What Is It Like to Be a Bat?" succinctly describes the problem: "Certainly it is possible for a human being to believe that there are facts which humans never *will* possess the requisite concepts to represent or comprehend. . . . Reflection on what it is like to be a bat seems to lead us, therefore, to the conclusion that there are facts that do not consist in the truth of propositions expressible in a human language. We can be compelled to recognize the existence of such facts without being able to state or comprehend them."[5] Arguing the inner life of bats or of animals in general is thus to argue something that human language is not equipped to express, perhaps like arguing the existence of the soul or of God.

Nagel's primary interest in his essay is not the bat's subjectivity, however. His concern is to refute reductive theories regarding the mind's relation to the body— theories that if we can know the brain in some measurable, material way, we can understand how the mind works. What is remarkable in his essay, however, is that the bat stands in no simple relation to or for a body. "It will not help to try to imagine that one has webbing on one's arms, which enables one to fly around at dusk and dawn catching insects in one's mouth; that one has very poor vision, and perceives the surrounding world by a system of reflected high-frequency sound signals; and that one spends the day hanging upside down by one's feet in an attic."[6] It will not help because the bat is more than a body, just as consciousness is understood to be more than the body, though nevertheless grounded in it.

Here Nagel stalls a tradition in Western philosophy that would align mind with "the human" and the body with "the animal." Aristotle, for example, wrote, "Where then there is such a difference as that between soul and body, or between men and animals, (as in the case of those whose business is to use their body, and who can do nothing better), the lower sort are by nature slaves and it is better for them as for all inferiors that they should be under the rule of a master."[7] Descartes identified the animal as mere body in order to show that animals functioned essentially as machines; "they have no reason at all, and . . . it is nature which acts in them according to the disposition of their organs, just as a clock, which is only composed of wheels and weights is able to tell the hours and measure the time more correctly than we can do with all our wisdom."[8] Although Nagel's choice of a bat reflects a modernization in the metaphor of machine such that animals may be said to have a complicated computer technology rather than a clock's spring mechanism, his point is that however alien the bat's body and physical habits, however much they may function like a computer, we cannot deny that "there is something it is like to be a bat." Bats have conscious experience, and if we humans have difficulty imagining that experience, the lack is our own. "I am restricted to the resources of my own mind," Nagel asserts, "and those resources are inadequate to the task."[9]

Erasing a human–animal divide along the lines of consciousness or subjectivity, Nagel puts the onus on us humans to recognize the limits of our own subjectivity, which is to say our own lack.[10] In this approach, his essay can also be understood as a counter to Heidegger's much cited distinction between the animal that is "poor in world" and the human who is "world forming." For Heidegger, in other words (and here he is in line with the humanist tradition), it is the animal that is lacking because "it" does not have language. Indeed, for him, the animal is a "that" and an "it," not a "who" or a "he or she" and, as such, is denied subjectivity. This denial and hence the animal's "poverty" are due to the animal's so-called lack of language because language is what affords humans access to things "as such." Speaking of a lizard basking in the sun on a rock, Heidegger writes that the "rock is not given for the lizard *as* rock . . . the sun in which it is basking is not given *as* sun."[11] The lizard is not able to inquire into the rock's or the sun's properties. The lizard has a relationship to the rock and sun, but that relationship is an impoverished one because the lizard cannot consider rocks or sun or warmth or comfort in the abstract way that language allows for. Understanding things as things, the world "as such," is the distinct property of human *Dasein*. This knowledge of things "as such" is another way of saying that *Dasein* is "world forming," able to abstract meaning from nature and apply it in varied contexts. To be world forming is to be a creator of culture, understood as a framework of symbolic meaning overlayed upon nature, a reconstruction of nature in the mind. This is the world in which humans dwell—one whose meaning is of our own creation. Nonhuman animals, for Heidegger, are considered to be unable to detach their consciousnesses from their environments in order to perceive them in any abstract way.

This view, which runs through philosophy and anthropology alike, can be critiqued from a variety of standpoints, including recent scientific research establishing that a variety of nonhuman animals participate in the creation and reproduction of culture.[12] Here I am less interested in such research undertaken to show how like humans nonhuman animals can be and more concerned with views that destabilize the view that we humans have of ourselves and of our world. Would it not be more appropriate, for instance, to say that knowledge of the rock or sun "as such" is specifically human knowledge, but not knowledge "as such." This criticism is similar to one raised by Elizabeth Costello in J. M. Coetzee's *The Lives of Animals*, who points out the blind spots of a long line of philosophers:

> Even Immanuel Kant, of whom I would have expected better, has a failure of nerve at this point. Even Kant does not pursue, with regard to animals, the implications of his intuition that reason may not be the being of the universe but on the contrary merely the being of the human brain. . . .
>
> Both reason and seven decades of life experience tell me that reason is neither the being of the universe nor the being of God. On the contrary, reason looks to me suspiciously like the being of human thought; worse than that, like the being of one tendency in human thought.[13]

• • • • • • • • • • •

Insofar as knowledge of things "as such" is knowledge arrived at through reason and language, must we not say that such knowledge is one tendency of human ways of knowing? That objects cannot be known independently of their perceiving subjects is at the center of the work of the German biologist Jakob von Uexküll, who takes over where Kant had his failure of nerve. Whereas for Kant the idea that a nonhuman animal can be understood to be a subject was unthinkable, for von Uexküll it is imperative not to address animals "merely as objects but also as subjects, whose essential activities consist in perception and production of effects."[14] Each and every animal constructs "its" own subjective universe, its *Umwelt*, in which objects are perceived and responded to according to the functional or perceptual signs or tones they emit for each individual subject.[15] Von Uexküll gives the example of a dog who has been trained to jump on a chair when given the command "chair." When the chair is removed and the command given, any other object on which the dog can sit assumes the meaning or "canine sitting tone" of "chair"—couch, crate, shelves.[16] There is no chair in itself. This is also true for humans for whom objects such as a stone can change meaning without changing their physical characteristics. The stone may mark a path or, when thrown, be marked as a missile or weapon. Because there are thus as many "worlds" as there are subjects, Uexküll describes each human and nonhuman animal as existing as if in a bubble that another subject may enter, but only at the risk that "all previous surroundings of the subject are completely reconfigured."[17]

Although Uexküll does distinguish between "simple" and "complex" or "multiform" environments in order to describe the relative number of objects and cues that may be meaningful for some animals (such as for the tick, who responds to only three stimuli or "carriers of significance": odor, temperature, and skin type), he also describes each world as perfectly self-contained and constructed for the security of its inhabitant. "All animal subjects, from the simplest to the most complex, are inserted into their environments to the same degree of perfection."[18] "Simple" would thus, for Uexküll, indicate a quantitative rather than a qualitative comparison. Whether the same may be true for Heidegger has been a matter of much debate. As Derrida describes in a close reading of Heidegger, the German philosopher alternately writes that animals are *"weltarm"* and *"weltlos"*: poor in world and without world. The former would seem to represent a comparative difference with human *Dasein* in terms of "privation" or "lack" of world. The latter implies a difference in kind or essence—no comparable world at all. As Derrida writes, "It is not that the animal has a lesser relationship, a more limited access to entities, it has an *other* relationship. . . . But the difficulties are already piling up between two values incompatible in their 'logic': that of lack and that of alterity."[19]

The significance of these two values becomes especially apparent with regard to the fundamental question for Heidegger: finding access to the essence of life, to the Being of beings. If animals are "poor in world," it is because, in Heidegger's view, they have limited access to Being "as such"; they do not and cannot question Being or life in the way that humans (and especially philosophers) do. However, if each and every animal (including human animals) lives in its own noncommunicating bubble, then we must assume we can have access only to the being of our own world and not to the being of others—including other animals. This is as much a privation for humans as it is for other animals.

In this respect, animals present us with the absolute problem of alterity—the difficulty or near impossibility of seeing or, perhaps even more so, hearing, smelling, sensing from the place of the absolute other. As Derrida emphasizes, Heidegger cannot or will not accede to a position, "however fabulous and chimerical it might be, that thinks the absence of the name and of the word otherwise, and as something other than a privation."[20] Indeed, Heidegger writes against a romantic tradition from Jean-Jacques Rousseau through Rainer Maria Rilke that would see human consciousness as an obstacle to a deeper knowledge of and oneness with the world, a oneness that is not doubled by the filter of self-consciousness.[21] This was Rousseau's dream in the "Fifth Reverie," when while he is out in his boat on the lake, all inward thoughts are stilled by the outward rhythms of the water. "The ebb and flow of the water, its continuous yet undulating noise, kept lapping against my ears and my eyes, taking the place of all the inward movements which my reverie had calmed within me, and it was enough to make me pleasurably aware of my existence, without troubling myself with thought."[22] In Rilke's "The Eighth Elegy," human consciousness, because of its dependence on representational thought, is similarly associated with alienation from Being or what he calls "the Open"—that which, he says, is "so deep in animals' faces." In fact, Rilke suggests that it is only through animals that we have any knowledge at all of "the Open."

> We know what is really out there only from
> the animal's gaze; for we take the very young
> child and force it around, so that it sees
> objects—not the Open, which is so
> deep in animal's faces.[23]

What Rilke thus privileges as an animal's ability to see beyond the phenomenal world Heidegger sees rather as instinctual "captivation" or more literally a state of benumbedness (*Benommenheit*) that has no possibility of opening the world "as world." According to Eric Santner, Heidegger downgrades the "uninhibited movement within the Open" that Rilke privileges to an "instinctual captivation (*Benommenheit*) by an environment," an "absorption in the *Umwelt*" that must be distinguished from the "intentional comportment within the openness of a *Welt*" that characterizes human reflection. In opposing *Umwelt* (literally the surrounding world) and *Welt* (understood as a world of our making), Heidegger seeks to distinguish "man's engaged absorption in a space of possibilities—in a historical form of life or *world*—from an animal's absorption in its *environment*."[24] Instinct/thought; captivation/historical agency; nature/culture—the distinction animal/ human cannot be made without recourse to an oppositional and anthropocentric thinking that essentializes both animal and human while ignoring the space of overlap between them.[25]

And yet, as Georgio Agamben points out in his deft reading of Heidegger, it is around the issue of captivation (understood as a kind of boredom) where Heidegger is most at pains to distinguish if not oppose animal instinct and human *Dasein* but is also confronted with a profound likeness between them. Humans are also riveted by things or beings that are not revealed to us, things that "refuse themselves," and this happens above all when we are bored. "Boredom brings to light the unexpected proximity of Dasein and the animal. '*In being bored, Dasein is delivered over* (ausgeliefert) *to something that refuses itself, exactly as the animal, in its captivation, is exposed* (hinausgesetzt) *in something unrevealed.'"*[26] In *The Fundamental Concepts of Metaphysics,* Heidegger devotes a number of chapters to a "profound" kind of boredom that he identifies with what he calls man's fundamental *"Stimmung,"* a word that has been translated as "mood" or "attunement." "Attunement" signals a state that is both emotional or psychological and physical; it is our (varying) capacity to be affected by or tuned by our environment and especially to be tuned or more emphatically "gripped" by that of which we are unaware. Boredom would thus reveal an animal attunement—a passivity or even vulnerability—at the core of *Dasein,* which, like the animal's "poverty in world," is synchronal with an inability to know that which affects it. Where human and nonhuman animals begin to separate is at the point where humans become aware of their boredom, where they wake up to the "not-open" of animal being within and without their human being. The difference for Heidegger, in other words, is that humans become aware of the animality they cannot know "as such."

Perhaps this begins to explain why animality or captivation is such a contested site—alternately regarded as what must be transcended in order to be human and what must be (re)discovered in order to truly know the Being of being or, more simply, what it means to be ourselves as human animals. Heidegger himself writes that "life is a domain which possesses a wealth of being-open, of which the human world may know nothing at all."[27] Efforts to know or to open up such wealth are fraught not only because the instruments of reason are inadequate, incommensurable with the coordinates of Being, but also because captivation and knowledge appear to be incompatible—one destroying the other. Attunement is not only that of which we are not conscious, but that which is destroyed by any attempt to be made conscious or thought. "Not only can an attunement not be ascertained," asserts Heidegger, "it ought not to be ascertained, even if it were possible to do so. For all ascertaining means bringing to consciousness. With respect to attunement, all making conscious means destroying, altering in each case, whereas in awakening an attunement we are concerned to let this attunement be as it is, as this attunement."[28]

Peeing and Time: Animality and the Aesthetics of Attunement
in Bill Viola's *I Do Not Know What It Is I Am Like*

How is it possible to awaken our attunement (and by extension our animality) without destroying it? An attempt to answer this question might be offered by Bill Viola's 1986 video *I Do Not Know What It Is I Am Like*. Those who are familiar with Viola's later works such as *Fire, Water, Breath* and *The Passions* might find the terms *attunement* and *captivation* more suited to describe these works' depictions of what David Ross calls "suspended states of awareness" in which mind and body are literally absorbed into environments of fire or water or distorted by emotional turmoil. In those later videos, the effect even for the viewer is, as Ross writes, "immersive—closer to that of floating under water than to watching a film."[29] Already in *I Do Not Know*, however, what can be called an "aesthetics of attunement" brings to light the extent to which what is often referred to as the "transcendent" or "sublime" of Viola's works is deeply grounded in the physical and sensate world that we share with animals. Described on the DVD jacket as "an epic journey into the inner states and animal consciousness we all possess" and conceived while Viola was an artist in residence at the San Diego Zoo, *I Do Not Know* links captivation to meditation and both to the power of the video camera to focus attention on what is unthought or on the elements that give rise to thought. In the words of the thirteenth-century Eastern spiritualist Rumi, whom Viola likes to quote, "You have seen the kettle of thought boiling over, now consider the fire."[30] Shot at the zoo, in wildlife preserves, and during a fire-walking ritual at a Hindu Temple in Fiji, the "fire" that Viola considers here is that of the bodies experiencing heat, wet, light, sound—bodies without which thought would not boil over. As Nagel asks of the bat, so Viola asks what it is like to be an embodied (animal) consciousness and attempts to render that experience through an intense state of witnessing made possible by the video camera.

One of the most memorable and unusual scenes of Viola's video is an inordinately long take of a buffalo urinating in a field. Seemingly unaware of the action that his or her body is performing even as this act clearly prevents that body from doing anything else, this buffalo might be the perfect representation of an animal's captivation, its

Buffalo. (From Bill Viola, "I Do Not Know What It Is I Am Like," 1986. Photo by Kira Perov. By permission of Bill Viola Studio.)

submission to a life of which it is unconscious. We may even ask if there is a subject of this action, if such bodily actions are those of a subject or, rather, as Descartes might insist, if they are simply mechanical reactions that bear no relation to consciousness. The difference between conscious or voluntary action and involuntary bodily reaction constitutes for Descartes the difference between being human and being animal. And yet we humans also spend much time performing involuntary bodily functions that we may learn to control but not dispense with, functions that serve no purpose other than merely to keep us alive. As Heidegger describes with regard to boredom, time during such functions becomes long or, as *Langweile*, the term for "boring" in German, suggests, long and drawn out. It is the ongoing time of the past or present perfect rather than the time of completed action. It is not the time that we plan, but because it may be habitual and recurrent, it is nevertheless the time that, like Heidegger says of the gaze of boredom, "penetrates us and attunes us through and through."[31] Viola thus confronts us with an experience of peeing and "being in time" that is at the intersection of animal captivation and human boredom.

From a slightly different perspective, to watch Viola's video and, in particular, to watch this act of the buffalo urinating are to be reminded that the grand metaphysical questions of time and consciousness cannot be considered independently of the bodies that allow them to be materialized, bodies that give them sensation, meaning, as well as duration. Such bodies, furthermore, are inseparable from the specific environments or "naturecultures" in which they develop and evolve. Unfolding in time, subjectivity is a function of the body and of the body's environment—a view that, we shall see, Viola both adopts and ironizes in the middle section of his video. As anthropologist Tim Ingold persuasively writes, "By taking the animal-in-its-environment rather than the self-contained individual as our point of departure—it is possible to dissolve the orthodox dichotomies between evolution and history, and between biology and culture."[32] Ingold develops what he calls a "dwelling perspective" in order to pursue Heidegger's deconstruction of an opposition between dwelling and building or between residing in the world and being "world forming." "We do not dwell because we have built," says Heidegger, "but we build and have built because we dwell, that is because we are dwellers. . . . To build is in itself already to dwell. . . . *Only if we are capable of dwelling, only then can we build.*"[33] When we are at home in our bodies, we can build homes in which we will find comfort and relief.

Dwelling, like captivation, emphasizes the inseparability of subjectivity, bodies, and environment. The first part of Viola's film brings us to gaze upon the impermanence of these relations as they unfold in time and toward death. Changes in weather, light, and sound register on bodies, whose tactile materiality is brought into sharp focus. As Catherine Russell writes, Viola's contemplation is "immersed in the transience of life. . . . He embraces mortality, violence, and decay as the means of transcending the existential divide between consciousness and nature."[34] But his is not a morbid view of death, not that anticipation that, according to Rilke, colors all experience of life such that "we, only, can see death."[35] The film displays severed heads and corpses in the fields, but they are not evidence of a past waiting to be written into history or transformed into meaning.[36] Rather, the corpse is viewed as corpse—nature or the real that resists history as it resists being drawn into narrative. Birds, flies, maggots disregard death to eat from its flesh. Ingold might say that history itself is recognized as a natural process, built upon a temporality of death, decay, and regeneration. To dwell in this time is to come to subjectivity not through language or historical agency, but simply through being a body in time. *I Do Not Know What It Is I Am Like* thus reminds us of the *what* that is at the foundation of every *who* and of the ways in which we humans try to distance ourselves from this *what*.

What am I like? The frustration of knowledge announced in Viola's title is immediately translated into a problem of perception. While an unidentified tribal music plays, camera work turns the world upside down and sideways for the viewer, and landscapes appear first outside and then reflected inside the lake waters, becoming their internal rather than external ground. As the music stops, the sounds of water lapping and dripping against unknown surfaces makes inside and outside, up and down, indistinguishable, as in Rousseau's boat dream, until we are literally shocked into blackout, only to emerge into a dark cavernous hole. Plato's cave may come to mind, reminding us again of the faulty nature of our perceptions, if not of the "irreality" of the images on the screen. More to the point, these images are images of a world that appears unknowable "as such": bulbous, wet objects may be read as coral or as pulsating body parts. In this first, introductory section of the film, we are as a child before a world whose meaning escapes us. We are drawn into it and long, perhaps, to touch and feel what is around us, and we are reminded that without a sense of self, without knowing "what I am like," I am unable to have a "meaningful" relation to the world around me. Jacques Lacan explains something similar in his essay "The Mirror Stage" when he writes that the child must have an image of self in order to relate in a meaningful way to his or her surroundings. One of the functions of the mirror, in other words, is to "establish a relation between the organism and its reality—or as they say, between the *Innenwelt* and the *Umwelt*."[37] That relation, however, is established through a sense of self that is deluded because the mirror (or the mother's look) reflects a false image of a unified and coordinated person who is able to master his or her environment. This act of self-recognition (or misrecognition, Lacan will go on to say) on the child's part is, moreover, one that Lacan contrasts with the gaze of a young monkey. "This act, far from exhausting itself as in the case of the monkey, once the image has been mastered and found empty, immediately rebounds in the case of the child in a series of gestures in which he experiences in play the relation between the movements assumed in the image and the reflected environment and between this virtual complex and the reality it reduplicates—the child's own body and the persons and things around him."[38] Where the monkey gives up and lets the image and *Umwelt* be, the child dramatically displays his (Lacan's pronoun) mastery over that environment and the objects in it.

Viola's film evokes not so much the monkey's recognition of the emptiness of self-image, but rather the consequences of its absence. Lack of self-confirmation results in an environment or *Umwelt* that cannot be mastered. As the camera emerges from the waters onto a field of grazing buffalo, the landscape appears blurred, moving in and out of focus, as if evaporating in the summer heat or as if the film itself, instead of securing a view, gives way to the elements of nature. When the film is clearly in focus, our attention is directed to a series of animal eyes and to their gaze that looks beyond the viewer without the possibility for meeting or, consequently, for recognition. The first eye is that of a dead buffalo—an eye we barely make out as eye through the voracious buzz of the flies around it. Our unimportance with respect to this eye and the process of nature in which it participates is emphasized again as the camera focuses in on the eyes of various birds and fish, none of which seems to see its viewers or to return our gaze. Video thus appears to join the countless institutions and technologies that fail to engage the animal's look. "At most," says John Berger, speaking of animals in zoo, "the animal's gaze flickers and passes on. They look sideways. They look blindly beyond."[39] This sideways look, he explains, is the ultimate consequence of their marginalization. "That look between animal and man, which may have played a crucial role in the development of human society, and with which, in any case, all men had always lived until less than a century ago, has been extinguished."[40] But is it *their* marginality or our own? Viola's evocation of nature's disregard for our look (if not for the sense of sight in general) would suggest the latter. How small indeed does the filmmaker appear when, apparently attempting to capture the animal's gaze, he comes to see his own reflection in an owl's eye. Rilke describes a similar sensation of being reflected in the eye of a black cat:

> as if awakened, she turns her face to yours;
> and with a shock, you see yourself, tiny,
> inside the golden amber of her eyeballs
> suspended, like a prehistoric fly.[41]

Neither empty nor masterful, that self-reflection comes to block our access to the animal's gaze, like Death or "World" that in Rilke's "Eighth Elegy" prevents humans from seeing what animals see, from seeing into "The Open"; "Always there is World."[42]

Ignoring or distancing himself from that "prehistoric fly" in the third section of the video, entitled "The Night of Sense," Viola moves fully into the artist's masterful gaze, here presented with a self-critical irony. Staring emotionlessly at the images he has filmed and now projects on a tiny video player, he replicates the tradition of picturing or the "world conceived and grasped as picture" that Heidegger critiques in his essay "The Age of the World Picture."[43] Heidegger links the growth of modern Western science to a new objectification of the world by and before a viewer who frames what is to be seen in order to study and measure that world according to human instruments of observation. Such instruments are made evident in the texts lying next to Viola's video player, texts on anatomy and on "stimulus and response." As such, picturing renders the world knowable in relation to the viewing subject standing outside it; there is no allowance made for the possibility that the world or, more specifically, I would add, the animals within that world might return the gaze or have a viewpoint of their own. Thus, for Viola the artist, the cat crying outside the artist's study is nothing more than a nuisance, not a fellow being to acknowledge.

Heidegger's "world picture," like Lacan's mirror stage, thus describes a similar dialectical and illusory relation between self and world through which the modern subject is born. As "man" frames and thereby creates a picture of the world, so does he become "the relational center of that which is as such"—in other words, the author

Owl. (From Bill Viola, "I Do Not Know What It Is I Am Like," 1986. Photo by Kira Perov. By permission of Bill Viola Studio.)

of the world and its contents.[44] "He" stands over it as its master, as what allows it to come into being. The discourse of science that Heidegger refers to is one that Viola clearly identifies with—it is the discourse that has produced those very masterpieces that Viola so often refers to in his videos and that is invoked in the still life of fish and wine glass set before the artist in this work. But as that still life turns into dinner, and Viola begins to carve into the fish flesh and eat it, we see also that this discourse has turned artworks into objects of consumption, whether for body or for mind. The potential violence of science and the complicity of video are evidenced at the end of this section and the transition to the fourth when a dog leaps to attack the camera, instigating what Catherine Russell has called "a nightmare of aggressive technology."[45] Strobes flash madly to the beat of loud, electronic pulses, revealing the briefest glimpses of landscapes, fire, live animals, dead animals, a zebra's stripes. The metaphorical resonances of what it means to shoot with a camera appear literalized.

• • • • • • • • • • • •

And yet just as Viola focuses on the places where extremes meet and become an unknowable in-between, so might it be that at the moments of its most aggressive violence the video camera also turns its own instrumentality upon itself, revealing its own power to engage the viewer viscerally, with no other objective than to dwell in this engagement with light, sound, and time. Whereas the third section begins by showing the destructive potential of a "modern" art form that confirms Enlightenment Man as center of a world that opens before him and for him, the fourth ends by revealing that same art form as one that turns back on the artist and viewer, destroying any certainty of point of view. As Russell writes, "Technology effectively becomes a representation of the limits of knowledge and vision."[46] We are captivated but unsure of what it is we see. Moreover, the very physical effects of Viola's camera work, rousing if not assaulting our eyes, our ears, and our very instinctive reactions to time and to pain, demonstrate to us not only that art engages a disembodied "free play of the imagination" (as Kant claimed), but that such play takes place in and through a body's involuntary perceptions. This body, the buzzards and maggots make clear, depends on its environment for sustenance.

The fifth and final section, "The Living Flame," appears at first to be the most ethnographic but is also the most visceral. Here the tribal music and drumbeats heard at various instances during the video come home to accompany a range of rituals performed by barely clothed men: fire walking, flagellation, and the slow piercing of folds of skin with skewers the size of kebabs. Intellectual distance is reduced to a minimum to make pain into a lived and not simply observed experience. Just as the first sections of the film have no frame, nothing to allow the viewers to locate where or what it is we are watching, so does this ethnography fail to give us any information or account of what or who is being filmed. Information is clearly not the point. Moreover, in its failure as ethnography this section brings us retrospectively to reevaluate the frustrated knowledge and vision of the earlier sections on animals. In the same sense that the fourth section is a failed ethnography, so is the first third of the film a failed anthropology—failed in that it offers no occasion for "Man" to recognize himself, even by recognizing what he is not. It is in this sense that Viola's footage works as much to jam "the anthropological machine" as to participate in it. Agamben uses the term the *anthropological machine* to refer to the process whereby the "human" is defined through opposition to or exclusion of what is nonhuman or animal. Ethnography has been one of the tools by which some humans are identified as more animal and less human, if not nonhuman. As Agamben explains with regard to a premodern taxonomy, *Homo sapiens* is an "optical machine" for producing man's recognition of himself. He "must recognize himself in non-man in order to be human."[47] But that machine must always focus on a fundamental likeness or what Agamben calls a "zone of indeterminacy,"[48] where the distinctions between human and nonhuman or human and animal are not so clear, where indeed they must be produced.

Recognition of the human is what Viola's film refuses from the beginning and in its very title. It refuses to participate in the anthropological project of separating *zoe* from *bios*, animal or bare life from political, historical, or, in this case, aesthetic life. Rather, it prefers to dwell in those spaces of betweenness or indeterminacy out of which such distinctions between animal and human, as between life and death, are produced. These spaces, moreover, are the ones that the anthropological machine would prefer to ignore. From peeing to possession rituals, Viola focuses on life as lived in present time, experienced rather than managed. Such experience can be understood only as an intense investiture in that animal life for its own sake, captivation with "captivation" in the sense of an animal that is "ecstatically drawn outside of itself in an exposure which disrupts it in its every fiber."[49] This physical exposure and response to one's environment is what we see in every flicker of the eye, cocking of the neck, and ruffling of the feather. These representations of "being in the world" do not depend on the separation of human and animal worlds, on nature and history. They do not represent Being as a project, but rather as the physical sensation of being alive and of being constantly drawn outside oneself to the environment and to the Other in that environment—whether that Other is predator, prey, or fellow traveler. If art or the artist that Viola himself represents has a project, then it might be understood more simply as "letting be"—to let be so as to be capable of being captivated by Being as by "bare life."[50]

In the final section or coda of the film, "letting be" is once again temporarily abandoned as we are brought to witness another masterful display of video technology. The camera dives into the water to scoop up a large fish that attaches to the lens as it flies into the air and soars above the landscapes revolving beneath. This fish, which recalls the fish in the previously viewed "still life," appears more still than ever and, indeed, dead against the revolving, moving landscape. In this literalized primacy of figure to ground, we might see an allegory of "the world picture" or of a Cartesian idea of vision as an operation of thought or "techne" that builds its own image of the world independently of that world. The ritual drumming heard during the film's previous section renders a stark contrast between that section's felt, physical intensity and this section's visual abstraction. The film, however, does not end here. The fish is brought gently to rest on its ground, from there to be immersed in "the soil of the sensible."[51] At this point, the music stops, as does the camera's movement, each replaced with the sounds and motions of nature, which reanimate the fish. No longer an object or symbol carved out of space, it becomes that which is reformed and reclaimed by the nature around it—flies crawl, and birds peck to slowly expose its flesh, then its bones. The appearance of a deer with head and ears cocked to focus on that which neither he (or she) nor we can see or know directs the viewer to the world beyond that of the camera, outside the frame. Rather than mastering time and form, the camera becomes the agent of deformation, accelerating so as to make visible the ravages of time and eventually the inevitability of disappearance.

Looking at Animals Looking: Frank Noelker's Critical Anthropomorphism

Let me return to Derrida's statement about thinking and his cat. "The animal looks at us, and we are naked before it. Thinking perhaps begins there." With this statement, Derrida unleashes his critique of a philosophical tradition that, if it has not ignored animals completely, has denied them subjectivity, the ability to look and to see. Realizing his shame before his cat, he is forced to realize that animals "have their point of view regarding me" and consequently that the demand for recognition that, according to philosophers from Hegel through Sartre, can come only from another man might come as well from another animal. And yet to focus on the gaze of the animal and especially on that of an animal who looks at me is to remain within a humanistic tradition that values sight above all other senses and that identifies seeing with knowing. We look at their look to see what they tell us about ourselves, what they see in us. This is anthropocentrism of another kind—one that critiques who is doing the picturing, but not the act of picturing itself.

Bill Viola addresses the idea of picturing by blurring or deforming the images we see so as to dismantle any sense of visual mastery over the seen world. Not only do we not see what an animal sees, but we cannot be sure of what, if any, knowledge comes from sight. As we must consider that our existence is marginal to their gaze, so must we consider that sight is marginal to their world, their *Umwelt*. But Viola's refusal to visualize what animals see may itself be a function of the very Enlightenment form of "picturing" that he critiques because picturing demands not only an objective and distanced view of the natural world, but also a view that avoids the charges of anthropomorphism. Although anthropomorphism was a common practice in earlier times, under the Enlightenment any attribution of our own capacities or characteristics to animals was seen to conflict with the scientific and rational capacities that made us human. The urge to identify with and so to anthropomorphize another's experience, like the urge to empathize with it, has been even more recently criticized as a form of narcissistic projection that erases boundaries of difference. And yet resistance to anthropomorphism can veer into what Frans de Waal calls "anthropodenial," a "willful blindness to the human-like characteristics of animals, or the animal-like characteristics of ourselves."[52]

Photographers and filmmakers seem currently more willing to risk the charge of anthropomorphism because of the moral stakes at hand. It is easier to care about those who are like us in some way than about those we can't fathom. Frank Noelker's recent series of chimp photographs, Chimp Portraits 2002–2006, present close-up headshots of chimpanzees who have been retired from lives as research subjects, entertainers, and pets. They are chimps who have lived their lives for us—injected with HIV, sold to roadside zoos, and transferred from cage to cage to be experimented on and examined as specimens. Noelker informs us of this past but photographs his subjects in a way to afford them all the dignity and stature of statesmen. They look intently and self-composedly at the camera.

The two-dimensional quality of Noelker's chimps contrasts with his earlier photographic work, Captive Beauty: Zoo Portraits, which, like Viola's film, focused on the "animal in its environment." But that environment is one fashioned wholly by humans, and as a result the animal's displacement and forced isolation are most noticeable and striking in the zoo photos. Giraffes peer above their bars against a backdrop of a painted desert; hippopotami drink under a brightly painted colonnade that frames a fake sky and is itself framed by cage doors. So out of place in such constructed environments, the animals seem barely real. Where Viola focuses on the animal's capacity for dwelling, what is evoked in these photos is the withholding of dwelling, the impossibility of being in the world rather than being beside or outside it. *Bored* is a word that has been used to describe these zoo animals, but it is important to distinguish this boredom from the notion of captivation that, for Heidegger, is also a kind of boredom. These zoo animals are captive to themselves not out of instinct, but because, like Rilke's panther, they have been robbed of their world and are held in ours instead.

> His vision, from the constantly passing bars,
> has grown so weary that it cannot hold
> anything else. It seems to him there are
> a thousand bars; and behind the bars, no world.[53]

As the photographic frame mimics the enclosed space of the cages, Noelker binds photography to other modern institutions or practices that would compensate for the loss of the animal in our society, but that, like zoos or pet keeping, become, as John Berger says, only monuments to that loss. "They [the animals] have been immunized to encounter, because nothing can any more occupy a *central* place in their attention."[54]

In Chimp Portraits, by contrast, Noelker attempts to revive that look. The term *portrait* seems incongruous for the images in Captive

Beauty; the individual animals are barely able to establish their identities against the habitats that engulf them. That is not the case for the chimps who are photographed in larger-than-life size, with full, frontal heads against an unidentifiable background. And in each portrait we come face to face or eye to eye with their gaze. Such photographs of chimpanzees may be at greatest risk of anthropomorphism, offering us the possibility for seeing ourselves in another species so like us. Noelker accentuates the anthropomorphic by focusing on the eyes—the heavy, soulful, and individualized gazes that he is so skilled at capturing. They look intently, and they look at us, turning their thoughtful, critical, and, some might say, almost human gaze upon us.

It is thus by very different means from what we saw in Viola's work that the act of looking is put under its own scrutiny in Noelker's portraits. Steve Baker has described a "balance of seeing and not-seeing" that has been used as a strategy in some documentary photography of animal abuse,[55] and Noelker seems similarly to give weight to what is not seen—to what is unseen or imagined. We see Tom and Roger and Kenya; we see the different shades and thickness of their fur, the different shapes and colors of their mouths, and above all their different expressions, showing them as distinct individuals. We are also given their stories, a context in which to interpret what we see on their faces, if not to see in them traces of the past. And we are surprised by how they appear unscathed. What we know of their pasts, of the horrific abuses they have suffered, remains invisible and is communicated only in an apparent translation: the text that accompanies each photo. Each of Noelker's chimps has his or her mouth closed as if to suggest that he or she will not or cannot speak to us. We have only "a report to the academy," as with Red Peter.

There is, of course, another reason for the closed mouths. The chimps look more controlled, more dignified, more human. This was a calculated decision on Noelker's part, a risk of anthropomorphism for the sake of the animal war in which anthropomorphism may have a valuable role to play. As some suggest, anthropomorphism is the first step to attributing mind to another being and, hence, to acknowledging an other as a subject capable of pain, pleasure, and will.[56] Noelker's strategy fits under the rubric of what I call "critical anthropomorphism." The individualized portraits do not simply elicit a response of

Tom. (Reprinted by permission of Frank Noelker.)

Roger. (Reprinted by permission of Frank Noelker.)

Kenya. (Reprinted by permission of Frank Noelker.)

sameness: "Look how like us they are" or even "Look how they must have suffered." Rather, his photographs, I would argue, force us also to wonder, "What do they see when they look at us?" "What must they think of us?" and, more important, "Who are 'we' who have done this to them?" In projecting sameness or similarity upon another species, we feel our gaze come back to us to make us question how well we really know who we are and whether we know what we are capable of.

In the work of Bill Viola and Frank Noelker, we thus witness two very different ways of looking at animals, two very different means of making visible something of "the animal" that has been unattended to, if not lost. Viola directs us first of all to bodies on land and in water, bodies that graze, breathe, and pee, in order to show us the "attunement" and vulnerability that we share with animals. Time is the ultimate master of us all, shaping and unshaping what it is *we* are like, even as it never allows us to know that likeness, whether from the regard of others or in ourselves. Vision itself is deprived of its mastery in the time-based medium of Viola's video art. What we come to see of the visible world is its impermanence. By contrast, the power of Noelker's photographs comes from the power of the gaze, even to the diminishment of bodily being. The question is not one of looking itself, but of who is looking and how.[57] The shock of his photographs is a function of the apparent humanity of these chimpanzees, who look and see and apparently know, even if they can't tell. They look at us in order to correct our vision so that we might act in accordance with what we see. As we see an animal who sees us, we confront a view of ourselves we may not have seen and, indeed, may not wish to see. We want to but should not look away.

Appendix: Biographies of Tom, Roger, and Kenya

Tom
Date of birth: unknown (196_?).

Tom was born in Africa. Taken from his family, he spent his first 30 years in the laboratory. Tom arrived at New York University's primate research facility, LEMSIP, on August 13, 1982, from the Buckshire Corporation at the age of about 15 years. In his subsequent 15 years at LEMSIP, "Ch-411" was knocked down over 369 times. Tom was inoculated with HIV in 1984 and for the rest of his time at the lab he was used mostly for vaccine research. Completely uncooperative in the lab, he was even knocked down for cage changes. After enduring some 56 punch liver biopsies, one open liver wedge biopsy, three lymph node, and three bone marrow biopsies, Tom gave up. Plagued constantly by intestinal parasites, he often had diarrhea and no appetite. When he had some strength, he banged constantly on his cage.

Roger
Date of Birth: 1980

Roger was born in a roadside zoo where he was pulled from his mother in his first year and sold to a family in Connecticut. When he was three the family sold him to circus trainers who traveled with Ringling Brothers Circus. He stayed in that situation until his handler died in 1993, at which time he was sold to another roadside zoo. There he was placed in the same cage with an adult male orangutan with only a chain link fence to separate them. At some point Roger was castrated. When he was eventually rescued there were considerable problems opening his cage, since the lock and even the door had corroded shut. It had been at least three years since he was out of his cage.

Kenya
Date of Birth: July 1, 1993

Kenya was pulled from her birth mother soon after she was born due to poor maternal care. After living in a human household in north Florida, she came to the Center when she was six months old and immediately began social interaction with other chimpanzees. She is very independent, exuberant, and gleeful … and she usually interacts with both humans and chimpanzees in a positive way.

Part II

. . . .

PET
TALES

3

. . . .

IS A PET
AN ANIMAL?
Domestication and Animal Agency

"Is a pet an animal?" asks Erica Fudge at the beginning of her insight-ful book *Animal*.[1] Much of contemporary theory would answer in the negative. "Anyone who likes cats or dogs is a fool," write Gilles Deleuze and Félix Guattari in *A Thousand Plateaus*.[2] For the latter, a dog or cat lover is a fool because the dog or cat is not really an animal, but a creature made by humans to confirm an image of ourselves we want to see, but one that, according to these authors, is restricting and regressive. Pets make us seem human when that means fulfilling an identity forced on us by our parents, our schools, and our gov-ernments, and it is the only identity, moreover, Deleuze and Guattari argue, that psychoanalysis understands. "We must distinguish three kinds of animals. First, individuated animals, family pets, sentimen-tal, Oedipal animals each with its own petty history, 'my' cat, 'my' dog. These animals invite us to regress, draw us into a narcissistic contemplation, and they are the only kind of animal psychoanalysis understands, the better to discover a daddy, a mommy, a little brother behind them."[3]

Real "animals" lie opposite of pets; they are, in Deleuze and Guat-tari's terms, the "demonic animals, pack or affect animals that form a multiplicity, a becoming, a population, a tale."[4] *Demonic* of course, is a term of value, if not endearment, for Deleuze and Guattari, signal-ing the power to be wild and unsocialized, to be deindividuated and multiple—a power of which, they claim, pets have been stripped. Pethood signals the animal's moral failing, an inability to channel those "intensities" and "affects" of internal movement and thus an inability to combat the need to conform to an identity imposed from the outside. As for Nietzsche, so for Deleuze and Guattari wildness signals both moral and physical health and thus the nobility that is sickened by the domestic pet.

And yet, Deleuze and Guattari maintain, it is possible for the pet to escape this fate, "possible for any animal to be treated in the mode of the pack or swarm; that is our way fellow sorcerers. Even the cat, even the dog."[5] But the outlook for pets has not been promising. Already in his seminal article of 1977, "Why Look at Animals," John Berger puts pet keeping side by side with zoos as institutions that make animals disappear. Pet keeping, he explains, force animals into a human, social setting that demands their deanimalization and eventually molds them into "creatures of their owner's way of life." "The small family living unit lacks space, earth, other animals, seasons, natural temperatures, and so on. The pet is either sterilized or sexually isolated, extremely limited in its exercise, deprived of almost all other animal contact, and fed with artificial foods. This is the material process which lies behind the truism that pets come to resemble their masters or mistresses."[6]

Berger's comments have found support in the work of historians Kathleen Kete and Harriet Ritvo. In *The Beast in the Boudoir*, Kete writes of the ways in which pet keeping in nineteenth-century Paris "mirrored and mimicked bourgeois culture," especially in its various attempts to mask and control animal "nature."[7] Thus, dogs were bathed, coiffed, and sometimes clothed; they were educated to restrain or display themselves appropriately, and their sexuality was tightly controlled so that when the time came, they could be mated (and indeed "married") with partners worthy of their well-bred (i.e., class) status. Focusing on Victorian England, Ritvo charts similar practices that led to the making of champion dogs and *The Stud Book*—a veritable who's who of canines—modeled on the pedigree that already existed for horses. Prizes for dogs, Ritvo emphasizes, were less an award for the animals themselves or even for their illustrious ancestry than for evidence of an owner's ability to "exploit" an animal's "physical malleability."[8]

These dogs were self-referential in that they proved the potential malleability and talent of the rising class of bourgeois pet owners.

Pets have become privileged examples of the potential, moral corruption of humans who regard nature as a resource to be exploited for personal and material gain. Yi-Fu Tuan's *Dominance and Affection: The Making of Pets* focuses on those moral processes that inspire or allow us to turn everything from plants to other humans into a servant, a companion, or a prized object. Whereas dominance alone produces a victim for whom there is little if any concern, Tuan argues, "dominance may be combined with affection, and what it produces is the pet."[9] As products of and subjects to the abuse of power, pets are potential victims, but their status, like the status of human–pet relations more generally, is rendered ambiguous because of the care and "humaneness" with which they may be bred, trained, and fed and because of the simultaneously abusive and productive ways power operates in the aesthetic–cultural realm. In the end, Tuan argues, "whether we use plants and animals for economic or playful and aesthetic ends, we *use* them; we do not attend to them for their own good, except in fables."[10]

This history of pets as objects of use, abuse, and exploitation follows a similar history of domestication that focuses on human agency and control over animals. Largely viewed with a Marxist lens, domestication has been understood to be a process of taming that turns animals into property. Anthropologist Juliet Clutton-Brock defines domestic animals as "bred in captivity, for purposes of subsistence or profit, in a human community that maintains complete mastery over its breeding, organization of territory and food supply."[11] In this history, which makes little distinction between animals used for food and animals for companionship (the latter believed to derive from animals used for protection or to keep other predators away), domestic is pitted against wild in a binary opposition of enslaved to free that carries a host of gendered, raced, and otherwise hierarchically organized associations. This view of domestication represents a reversal—at once romantic and politically charged—of Enlightenment taxonomies such as Thomas Bewick's *General History of Quadrupeds*, where tamable or trainable animals were at the top of a hierarchy, tame was on a continuum with civilized, and wild was most often associated with savage or sometimes, by association, with unruly lower classes in need of a master to discipline or defend them.[12]

The term *domestic*, as Richard Bulliet reminds us, was first used for animals in 1620 and comes from the Latin *domus*, signifying "living in or belonging to a household."[13] By the end of the eighteenth century, this process of moving into the house would take on negative associations of effeminacy and the loss or weakening of natural strength. Thus, for example, in imagining what humans would have been like in a state of nature, Rousseau considers that "the horse, the cat, the bull, even the Ass . . . have a sturdier constitution, greater vigor, force, and courage in the forests than in our homes; they lose half of these advantages when they are Domesticated, and it would seem that all our care to treat and to feed these animals well only succeeds in bastardizing them. The same is true of man himself: As he becomes sociable and a Slave, he becomes weak, timorous, groveling, and his soft and effeminate way of life completes the enervation of both his strength and courage."[14]

From Rousseau through Nietzsche to Deleuze and Guattari, we find a similar condemnation of the domestic pet as a deanimalized creature that has been stripped of its original virile wildness and tamed into a "feminine" and inauthentic servitude. Domestication is understood to be a process done to animals by humans through coercive means. But because, as Rousseau suggests, domestication is also something that humans did to themselves and not always wittingly, not necessarily out of that "property of being a free agent" by which a human is distinguished from an animal, but out of those passions that are shared with animals and that turn habits into needs, he leaves open the possibility that other animals may also, if to a lesser extent, have participated in the process.[15] Could animals have "chosen" domestication, as the title of Steven Budiansky's *The Covenant of the Wild: Why Animals Chose Domestication* suggests?[16]

What it means to be an actor in history and what it means to have agency in the historical process are notions that have been deconstructed since the 1950s, whether from the standpoint of linguistic or psychoanalytic or cultural theory. We humans are shaped by language, by the unconscious, and by the world around us as much as we shape and create that world. To realize that history is not only the result of conscious intentionality is also to open the door to understanding that animals might also have agency in certain historical processes. Indeed, to realize that historical agency should not be regarded only in terms of human intention has been crucial to recent reexaminations of the process of domestication and the role of humans and animals alike. As Philip Armstrong explains, agency has become a problematic topic within animal studies because a notion of nonhuman agency carries the charge of anthropomorphism. But responses from human–animal geographers such as Chris Philo and Chris Wilbert, says Armstrong, "turn the charge of anthropomorphism on its head" by explaining that the "allegation of anthropomorphism itself derives from an anthropocentric and ethnocentric understanding about what agency is." Taking the lead from Philo and Wilbert, Armstrong writes that the assumption that agency as a "capacity to effect change" requires rational thought and conscious intention derives from "an Enlightenment humanist paradigm within which these traits came to define the human as such."[17]

In this respect, it is significant that Rousseau was already writing in the eighteenth century against such a paradigm that regards intention as the motor of history (and, hence, domestication). Rousseau ultimately believed that it is impossible to know what allowed humans to separate from the state of nature, if indeed such a state ever existed. Almost a hundred years later, as Bulliet emphasizes, Darwin believed that the "origins of domestic species would always remain obscure."[18] Because of the difficulty of understanding how humans could have knowingly domesticated a species without having prior knowledge of the results, the Marxist framework that regards domestication as a process of intentional shaping and oppression has become less tenable. Bulliet argues that, "in most cases, domestication came about as an unintended, unremembered, and unduplicatable consequence of human activities intended to serve other purposes."[19] Some biologists, such as Raymond Coppinger, have argued that "the dog domesticated itself" through forces of natural selection that gave an advantage to those most adept at scavenging from human garbage.[20] The thesis published by Lynn Margulis in 1966 that symbiosis is a driving force of evolution, despite its initial rejection by mainstream biologists, has recently become a central idea of evolutionary biology.[21] Drawing on these biological models, anthropologists have promoted a model of coevolution that views domestication as a symbiotic and dynamic relationship between humans and animals independent of either's forethought or conscious intent and that potentially ascribes agency to both.[22]

Such a shift in the debates reflects a similar shift in attitudes toward anthropomorphism and its role in how we understand the process of domestication. If, that is to say, the effort to avoid accusations of anthropomorphism led theorists to discount agency and intention in animals, the twin wrong of "anthropodenial" might be said to have encouraged others to reconsider if not intention, then the subjective desires and emotions of certain animals that could also lead them into a domestic relationship. Anthropodenial, as Frans de Waal has characterized it, is "the *a priori* rejection of shared characteristics between humans and animals . . . [a] willful blindness to the human-like characteristics of animals or the animal-like characteristics of ourselves."[23] As archaeologist Gala Argent concludes in her work on the domestication of horses, the domination model of horse–human relations focuses on the exploitation and use of animals by humans, underestimating those "social needs . . . for inclusion and affection" that are shared by humans and horses alike.[24]

Such focus on the dynamic force of affective relations has been especially pronounced in recent thinking about relations between pets and their humans. Because pets live with us and offer the opportunity to observe and interact with their behavior, historian Keith Thomas has argued that pets and their keepers have played a crucial role in challenging dominant philosophical and scientific views concerning animal emotions, intelligence, and the human monopoly on notions of personhood, thought, and subjectivity.[25] Many municipalities in the United States have recently changed the legal terminology from *pet owners* to *pet guardians* in order to reflect the change in pets' status from property to companions with individual needs that must be met. Concomitant with the reevaluation of the origin, the process, and consequently the ethics of domestication has been a reconsideration of practices associated with pet keeping and, in particular, the art and sport of animal training. As I discuss in chapter 8, training takes center stage in the work of Vicki Hearne and Donna Haraway, both as a real

· · · · · · · · · · · ·

and daily practice of sustained interaction with another animal and as a metaphor for a practice of language and world building in which humans and other animals participate equally in establishing verbal, gestural, and sensory communication. For Haraway and Hearne, training is what allows a pet to escape the status of victim by offering a means of communication between species. Training sets up a relation between unequals—animals of unequal lexicons and unequal capacities for scent, touch, and hearing—but each of whom must be acknowledged as "having a world" and having something to say. For training to work, each must become attuned to the language of the other, while acknowledging that there will be limitations to knowing that other.

Whereas Hearne approaches training from within the philosophical tradition of skepticism, in which humans are shorn of their certainty about themselves and about the world, Haraway looks at it from a science studies perspective influenced by biological theories of coevolution and actor–network theory. Training institutes "contact zones" between species similar to those zones that Mary Louise Pratt defines between cultures: "social spaces where cultures meet, clash, and grapple with each other."[26] For Hearne, such spaces provide for new kinds of languages—pidgin languages that are at once embodied and arbitrary in the linguistic sense, but that inspire and depend on an interspecies trust or moral certainty that human languages cannot provide. For Haraway, such contact zones are of scientific and historical significance, proving that "co-constitutive companion species and coevolution are the rule, not the exception."[27] In other words, cooperation or at least codependency rather than competition in the Darwinean sense may be the motor of evolution. Humans and animals are entangled with each other at the microbial and ontological levels such that each becomes what it is only by virtue of that entanglement where what is a product of "nature" cannot be separated from what is a product of "culture." For Hearne and Haraway, training, as one form of entanglement in which humans and animals clash and grapple but also find something they mutually enjoy, is not an anthropocentric exercise of power over an animal that depends on submission and obedience to a human-authored design, but rather an intersubjective relation that demands an openness to difference on both sides and an openness to be transformed by difference.

What of those who beat a dog or horse into submission and who force it to act out of fear? The point is, as Rebecca Cassidy writes, that domestication is an "ongoing relationship" that "may be exploitative or mutual, intentional, or serendipitous."[28] Even Deleuze and Guattari concede that "even the cat, even the dog" may be treated in "the mode of the pack" or in a way that fosters its "multiplicity."[29] Some theories are bent on proving humans' inhumanity toward animals, but in so doing they disregard or dismiss animals' humanlike qualities. Other theories focus precisely on the unseen or unacknowledged capabilities that pets share with humans in an effort to redeem practices that rely on those qualities, if not exploit them. Full disclosure: I keep dogs and ride horses, and my defense of these practices is not disinterested. But the alternative of seeing dogs and cats and horses only as products of indefensible human dominion is also ideological.

In chapters 4 and 5, I look at literary representations of pets that suggest a range of relationships with their humans. These fictions are themselves contact zones in which struggles with otherness are played out and worked through or not. Of course, humans have the last word in these representations because, as far as we know, our pets are not able to write or read (a point that Virginia Woolf makes with regard to Elizabeth Barrett's dog Flush), but that does not mean that real animals have had no share in those representations. Indeed, just as our representations can have real effects in the world by shaping how we understand other animals and thus how we might relate to them, so those animals and in particular the animals we live with affect the way we represent them or their literary surrogates. In his work on animals in film, Jonathan Burt writes of the "unintended effects" often produced by an animal on screen and of the "mutual gaze between human and animal" that allows us to speak about the way in which an animal "does regulate its symbolic effects."[30] In literature, of course, that gaze is filtered through words, but it is possible to speak of the unintended effects on narrative that are produced by dogs or horses who, according to Vicki Hearne, have their own stories about what, for example, fetching a ball or being caught might mean. And their stories, if we acknowledge them, can induce us to change ours.[31]

The stories I have chosen might be classified as modernist fictions or works by modernist authors, but my argument here is less about modernist literature than about the prevalence and importance of pets in modernity, a historical fact that may or may not be causally linked to modernism or postmodernism.[32] Recent works on animals in modernist literature have focused especially on issues of human "animality," especially as a result of the prominence made of this fact in Darwin and Freud's writings. Here I am concerned with the fact of human animality only insofar as it becomes apparent in relation to one's dog or cat or horse, which is to say as a result of a relation to an animal we live alongside and not only to the animal we harbor within. I likewise do not attempt to trace broad cultural shifts in our relations to domestic animals, whether because of industrial capitalism (for which animals exist only as resources) or because we live in a post-domestic society (and thus have lost experiences of animal life and death that may have been familiar to our parents' or grandparents' generation), although I find each of these shifts to be significant and their characterizations regarding human–animal relations to contain unavoidable truths.[33] The problem, however, is not only that such attempts to "account for the key changes [in these relations] (anti-cruelty legislation, animal protection, animal rights, the civilizing of manners) . . . have failed to take stock of continuities or changes that lead in the opposite direction," as Adrian Franklin attests,[34] but also that taking into account specific social or economic locations within cultures and history, as Franklin proposes, does not provide for the shifts that one individual may undergo in a lifetime and even in a split second. Ontogeny does not recapitulate or confirm phylogeny.

What I am especially interested in here is the individual pet–human relation and how that relation participates in and affects our under-standing of a modern sense of self—as human and animal. Individual identity is represented as a problematic concept in the literature of modernity, where markers of class, race, gender, sexuality, and even species have become unstable and uncertain and where the sense of self that those markers are said to reflect (and at times produce) is in constant need of affirmation and support. Because pets are part of our private, interior life (and, for some of us, part of our public, professional life), because we live with them, they offer one means to affirm and project identity—witness the number of celebrities, presi-dents, and Facebook members photographed with their dogs. But just as, in Hearne's view, dogs and horses often reject the stories we tell about them, so may they reject the stories that we tell about ourselves. We may put up a counterresistance, in which case the asymmetry of domestic relations almost always works to the animal's disadvantage, if not leading tragically to their deaths; Thomas Mann's "Tobias Mindernickel" offers an example of this plot. Or we may grow ever more attuned to their own pidgin languages such that our life narratives follow plots that they are in part responsible for and for which we are grateful to them. Thomas Mann's later novella *Man and Dog* and Virginia Woolf's *Flush* offer versions of this story.

4

· · · · · · · · · · · · · · · · · · ·

GENDERED
SUBJECTS/ABJECT
OBJECTS
Man(n)'s Best Friend

My dog.—I have given a name to my pain and call it "dog": it is
just as faithful, just as obtrusive and shameless, just as entertaining,
just as clever as any other dog—and I can scold it and vent my bad
moods on it, as others do with their dogs, servants and wives.

—Friedrich Nietzsche, *The Gay Science*, trans. Walter Kaufmann

What belongs to greatness.—Who will attain anything great if he does
not possess the strength and the will to *inflict* great suffering?

—Friedrich Nietzsche, *The Gay Science*, trans. Walter Kaufmann

Shame on You, Tobias

In her book *Melancholia's Dog*, Alice Kuzniar asks whether the feeling of shame blurs the boundary between humans and animals in the
very act of constructing it.[1] The feeling of shame, according to Freud
and Lacan, is what separates humans and animals, but shame is experienced, Kuzniar suggests, at the moment we act most naturally or
most "animal like"—as if to experience shame were " to feel improper
or unnatural at doing something natural."[2] Like shame, abjection is a
state that similarly reveals our animality in the moment we most wish
to distinguish ourselves from it. Shame might be regarded as the conscious (if unwilled) manifestation of the unconscious or unacknowledged state of abjection. Both abjection and shame are states of confusion or dissatisfaction about who or what the self is, who or what I

am. As Julia Kristeva writes, "I experience abjection only if an Other has settled in place and stead of what will be 'me.'"[3] This Other is often conceived of as animal or as body—that which has yet to be civilized or cultured—but is really a facet of the self that I do not recognize or do not yet know. Abjection unsettles the boundaries between me and not-me or between me and my group or kin and forces me to separate myself from it, sometimes violently, in order to affirm who I am. In abjection, as Kelly Oliver explains, there is "another animal lurking behind the origins of humanity, a darker, more frightening beast, our dependence on which we disavow and abject."[4]

Thomas Mann's early story "Tobias Mindernickel" tells the tale of an abject man— an "odd" and "quite ridiculous" man whose appearance and clothes are the brunt of neighborhood cackles and contempt.[5] An outcast among men, Tobias also seems unaware of what others think and greets those who laugh at him with "humble courtesies." Indeed, it appears that he recognizes his sorry state only when he witnesses it in another. This recognition occurs first after having witnessed a young boy injure himself. He immediately approaches the boy with "words of consolation": "Have you hurt yourself? . . . How miserable you look lying there . . . How I feel for you" (4). Following the episode with the boy, Tobias offers similar aid to a frightened dog who is being sold on the street. His relationship with the dog becomes the focus of the story.

An outsider who empathizes with those (human and nonhuman) like him, Tobias might first appear to the reader like Rousseau's "savage man" whose "commiseration" with those who suffer is all the stronger because of his closeness to a "state of nature," which is described also as a state lacking self-reflection. I quote Rousseau at length because the opposition he describes between the state of nature and the state of philosophy (which is a state of reflection) is part of the intellectual tradition that Mann responds to throughout his work.[6]

> Indeed commiseration will be all the more energetic in proportion as the onlooking animal identifies more intimately with the suffering animal: Now this identification must, clearly, have been infinitely closer in the state of Nature than in the state of reasoning. It is reason that engenders amour propre, and reflection that

reinforces it; . . . reason that turns man back upon himself; reason that separates him from everything that troubles and afflicts him: it is Philosophy that isolates him; by means of Philosophy he secretly says, at the sight of a suffering man, perish if you wish, I am safe.[7]

For Rousseau, identification with suffering comes more easily in the state of nature. As we grow up and become "human"—understood in Enlightenment terms—we lose that possibility for pity and empathy even as we gain the possibility for philosophy. Philosophy offers us ideas with which we may separate ourselves from others and even protect ourselves from (or abject) their suffering, and at the same time it allow humans to define themselves as intellectual or reasonable beings rather than as suffering and feeling ones. In Mann's story, alternatively, the title character becomes human through empathy with a suffering animal. But the story is also a frightening parable of empathy gone wrong, of empathy with suffering that becomes so necessary for this human's sense of self that he, himself, must inflict suffering on the animal in order to share in it and earn his humanity.[8] Tobias is a man for whom the lack of self-love, if not of philosophy, has savage consequences.

More noble savage than gentleman, Tobias is a creature unfit for society. Although well groomed and clean, his clothes are either too tight or too short and offer no protection from the elements. Most peculiar is the quality of his gaze—like a prey animal, he "continues to glance around in fear and scurry along his way," and, the narrator suggests, he "seems to lack that natural sovereignty of sensory perception that allows the individual to gaze out upon external phenomena" (2). On the one hand, his sorry and lonely state might be, the narrator offers, the result of life's hardships, but on the other hand "it's quite possible . . . that he's simply unequal to the task of being a man." Indeed, to infer from his state of " tortured submissiveness," one would more readily believe that he is a throwback of natural selection: "nature has denied him the strength, equilibrium and spine necessary to exist with his head held upright" (3).

It is with some surprise, then, that we find that at the moment when Tobias displays that sense of natural commiseration, going out of his way to console and bandage the bloodied head of the "poor boy" who had tripped while running, he is also able for the first time to stand "firm and upright" (4). The repeated term *upright (aufrecht)* carries implications both of becoming human and becoming erect, the two linked by their mutual arousal from the boy's wounded vulnerability. This human's sublimated sexuality thus offers a different gloss on Foucault's description of the emergence of the homosexual as "a species" at the turn of the twentieth century, not long after Darwin's explanations for the origin of species.[9] When Tobias buys the young dog in the marketplace a few days later, the complicated and prohibited relations between outlaw sex and species are brought into focus. One might read the story as the attempt to reject this awakened and outlaw sexuality, similar to what happens in the Poe and Maupassant stories I discuss later. But a more accurate view, I believe, is to see Tobias's wanting to maintain the "uprightness"—his humanity or masculinity or both—he has enjoyed and recognizing that he can do so only by keeping the dog in a state of suffering and fear. The result is a story of sadomasochistic, domestic violence that is painful to read. In other terms, "Tobias Mindernickel" pits Hegel's master/slave dialectic against a Christian ethos of pity and suffering in order to stage the process of becoming human through the struggle for recognition, played out in the volatile relations between a man and his willful dog.

Inquiring into the names given in this story reveals complicated origins and twisted significance. Tobias is the name of a young boy and dog owner in the biblical Book of Tobit. According to the version of this story based on St. Jerome, the young and pious Tobias is sent on a journey by his father to collect payment owed to the father. He is accompanied by his dog, who is represented as his faithful companion and friend—one of the only positive references to dogs in the Hebrew Bible. Indeed, the story was never admitted into the Jewish canon—perhaps another instance of a long-standing Jewish antipathy to dogs.[10] In Mann's story, Tobias nevertheless gives his dog a Hebrew name, Esau, from the Book of Genesis. The story of Jacob and Esau, like Mann's story of Tobias and Esau, is a tale of deception and struggle for authority. Esau, Jacob's red-headed and hairy twin brother, arrives home famished from working the fields and is talked into selling his birthright to his younger brother for a plate of red lentil stew. In Mann's story, it is Tobias who takes advantage of his dog's hunger, offering Esau a plate of boiled beef in exchange for giving obedience to Tobias. Esau the dog is initially receptive to this offer, responding to his name and to Tobias's various commands. But he eventually grows tired and bored of the game, with the result that Tobias, having discovered the joy in having his commands obeyed, is seized by an "irrational" and "indignant rage" at the dog's unwillingness to be subdued and takes to mercilessly beating him. Only at the sight of the dog's humbled and "beseeching eyes" does his rage turn to pity and to the melancholy happiness of taking care of him. A pattern is thus set up that exposes Tobias's dependence on the dog's suffering for his own pity and pleasure—if not for confirming who he is and wants to be. After the beatings and the accidental but deep wound from a bread knife, Tobias finds "happy relief" in empathizing with the "poor little creature," keeping Esau inside the house with him and speaking to him with "pitying words" that show he feels the dog's pain. The end of the story is all too apparent to the reader, even though the narrator writes that it is so "incomprehensible and dastardly" that he can't recount it in detail. He tells enough of the long knife wound deep in the dog's chest to make the reader cringe in horror and sympathy with the dog, but also in a perverse sympathy or identification with Tobias, who "had laid his face down upon Esau's body and was crying bitterly" (10).

Where, we might ask, does Mann position himself in this story that, the narrator admits, cannot be told in full? Its ending recalls another story told about Nietzsche at the end of his life, when in 1889 he is said to have flung his arms around the neck of a horse who had been beaten by a cab driver.[11] The Nietzsche incident, often said to mark the beginning of the philosopher's fall into psychosis, in turn recalls a moment in Fyodor Dostoevsky's *Crime and Punishment* (which Nietzsche had read two years earlier) when Raskolnikov has a fateful dream in which a young boy witnesses the beating death of a horse by an enraged cart driver. Beside himself, the boy "pushed his way, shrieking through the crowd to the mare, put his arms round the dead muzzle dabbled with blood and kissed the poor eyes and mouth."[12] In each of the stories, there is an identification between beater and beaten. In "Tobias," the man who is beating the dog and the boy who is crying over the beaten animal body are the same person.

In Dostoevsky, the positions of beater and beaten are further identified with the sympathetic onlooker through the dreamer, Raskolnikov himself. With "his whole body feeling bruised" upon waking, Raskolnikov questions if he will really take the axe and beat, not a horse or dog, but an old lady. A horse is being beaten, a dog is being beaten, a child/old lady is being beaten; in each instance there is a shifting and substitutability of positions: somebody is beaten, somebody watches, somebody beats—and that somebody is the same person.[13]

"The question is not Can they reason?, nor, Can they talk? but, Can they suffer?" wrote Jeremy Bentham in 1789 regarding the moral basis on which to ground our treatment of animals.[14] But on what grounds do we identify suffering? How might our reason, as Rousseau suggested twenty-five years earlier, be a hindrance to identifying suffering in another or to moving beyond identification to acts of relieving it? The story of Jacob and Esau is the story of a calculating man whose cunning takes advantage of his ruddy, appetitive, and animalistic older brother. As Robert Alter writes regarding Jacob's "legalistic calculation," "Perhaps this is a quality needed to get and hold onto the birthright, but it hardly makes Jacob sympathetic and moral ambiguities will pursue him in the story."[15] Mann's story suggests that our reason may stand in the way of kindness, that sharing suffering rather than being able to relieve it may result from a weakness in our reason, a weakness in our philosophy, as Nietzsche, too, experienced. It is reason or, as Rousseau said, "philosophy that isolates." Philosophy may allow us to say to a suffering man or animal (although "secretly," Rousseau says, as if our "humanity" would be otherwise against such reasoning), "Perish if you wish, I am safe." But this statement may do less harm than the irrational and unconscious fantasies we project onto our domestic animals even as we empathize with their suffering. Mann, we know, had read Nietzsche as early as 1894 and was greatly influenced by his writing,[16] but his perspective on Nietzsche's morality was often ambivalent, perhaps like Nietzsche's own perspective.[17] Having claimed that "the suffering of others infects us, pity is an infection,"[18] Nietzsche himself could be overwhelmed by pity "for the horse" or, in Roland Barthes's description, "gone mad for pity's sake."[19] Perhaps we must be cautionary about the morality of pity in either of its romantic manifestations, whether we think of it as that which, according to Rousseau, has been lost in society or that which, according to Nietzsche, is the sickness of the domesticated, social being. "Pity," Nietzsche wrote, "makes suffering contagious."[20]

Empathy and Madness: Poe's Cat, Maupassant's Horse

If I read "Tobias Mindernickel" as a cautionary tale about pity and empathy,[21] I run counter to a current trend that has regarded the faculty of empathy as everything from an important historical tool to the stuff of good literature ("the sympathetic imagination") or, more important for our purposes, as the origin and basis for an ethical relating to animal others.[22] Even from the start, empathy may be a problematic concept to apply to human–animal relations if it is true, as some believe, that the object of empathy—or sympathy, which is said to share the same "moral universe"—is "humanity."[23] In other words, empathy may be anthropocentric at its core—asking us to acknowledge a shared humanity in an animal even to the extent that such a value may, historians suggest, have become ethically suspect in the twentieth century. This problematic is one that philosophers of ethics are grappling with, wondering to what extent a cognitive form of empathy that is trained and educated to account for an animal's different world may overcome the limitations of affect or feeling.[24] In an effort to avoid charges of anthropomorphism, thinkers such as Kenneth Shapiro speak of "kinesthetic empathy," and Ralph Acampora theorizes what he calls a "transpecific conviviality . . . on the level of bodiment" in order to avoid constriction to " a homo-exclusive horizon."[25] But even if we are able to acknowledge that we share soma with the more-than-human world, what is it that guarantees the ethical status of our somatic drives?

Before Freud developed the idea of the unconscious as a place for the animal within the human, writers such as Mann, Dostoevsky, Maupassant, and Poe were making connections between violent, irrational drives and an animal state not in terms of a metaphorical animality, but in relation to the dogs, horses, and cats who, as domesticated beings, are part of everyday life. As in "Tobias Mindernickel," so in Edgar Allan Poe's "Black Cat" and Guy de Maupassant's "Fou?" (Crazy?) encounters with pets stimulate heretofore unseen and "mad" aspects of the protagonists' own lives and thereby raise questions concerning their own "domestication," what it serves and to what effect. Poe's protagonist is much like Tobias in that he is initially described as both peculiar and sympathetic, his sympathy directed especially toward animals. "From my infancy I was noted for the docility and humanity of my disposition. My tenderness of heart was even so conspicuous as to make me the jest of my companions. I was especially fond of animals, and was indulged by my parents with a great variety of pets. With these I spent most of my time, and never was so happy as when feeding and caressing them."[26] And it is that very softness that turns "perversely" against its own object of affection, bringing the narrator to commit a series of violent acts against his "own nature" and his cats.

Madness, of course, is a limitation of our ability to choose our actions and thus an affront to the notion of free will that, since Aristotle, has distinguished humans from animals. In a discussion of perversity in Poe, Stanley Cavell suggests that Poe raises the skeptics' questions such as "Am I alive or dead?" and "Am I a human being or a monster?"[27] Even beyond the either/or, Poe asks: "Can I be mad and still be human?" In an attempt to answer that question in the affirmative, the narrator of "The Black Cat" destroys the creature who raises those doubts—the cat who appears more free, more sane, certainly more able to love, and thus more human than the narrator. Poe's view on the "metaphysical suspicion" regarding existence thus flies in the face of Cavell's moral insistence that we accept the "claim of others as the price of knowing or having one's existence."[28] Poe—or at least Poe's narrator—asserts the denial or annihilation of the other as that price.

Maupassant's short story "Crazy?" raises a similar problematic in which the narrator's madness and thus "manhood" are brought into doubt by his rivalry with a horse. Here the "claims of the other" are evident both in the narrator's lover, who no longer responds to his efforts to excite or arouse her, and in her horse, who, he realizes, has taken his place.

> Every morning at dawn she took off at a gallop, over the plains and through the woods; and each time she would return languid, as after frenzies of love.

. . . .

I understood! I was jealous of the nervous and galloping horse; jealous of the wind that caressed her face when she gave into an impulsive ride; jealous of the leaves which kissed her ears in passing; of the drops of sun that fell on her forehead between the branches; jealous of the saddle that carried her and that she squeezed with her thighs.[29]

Empathy here inflames envy as the narrator feels himself into her excitement, only to heighten the ignominy of his absence from it and its cause. Resolving to take vengeance, he prepares himself as if he "were to fight a duel." Rigging a trap that trips the horse and rider, he then places one of his pistols in the horse's ear and, "like a man," kills it .[30]

In a final twist, Maupassant's story recalls Poe's in a manner that reveals the gendered violence of acting "like a man." When Poe's narrator attempts to kill the cat, his wife intervenes, but only to succumb to the blow of the axe. Similarly, as Maupassant's narrator finds himself whipped by his lover for his actions, he shoots his last bullet into her stomach. The story's final imperative, "tell me if I am crazy," calls upon the reader's empathy—empathy that would be felt, we must assume, only by one who knows what it is like to have one's manhood put into doubt. In these stories, in other words, manhood is sought through the joint sacrifice of women and animals. That these pets are so-called "humanized animals" does nothing to grant them a status of exception to the sacrificial structure that, as Derrida shows, grounds human subjectivity.[31] Carrie Rohman writes of the resonances between Derrida's sacrificial structures and Judith Butler's "discursive exclusion" such that becoming human is a process encoded both by the abjection of the animal (to be human is to be not-animal and, for Poe and Maupassant, not mad) and "through the cultural norm of gender."[32] The normative male subject would then come to be defined as not-woman—hence, the need to destroy the woman and her claim on the subject.

Man(n) and Dog

Let me return to Cavell's conjecture regarding the price we pay for trying to know or to own our existence. In the stories discussed earlier, we saw that the cost is annihilation of the other who has claims on me, but paying this cost only succeeds in buying the stamp of madness rather than certainty. Twenty years after Mann wrote "Tobias Mindernickel," he wrote a novella entitled *Herr und Hund* (*Man and Dog*), which would appear to illustrate an alternative pathway to knowledge of the self. In it, the narrator—a man apparently of secure means and reputation—has his world thrown into question by his dog.[33] But this story bears the mark of Cavellean comedy rather than tragedy because the narrator is "touched by" but not "done in" by others' problems.[34] *Man and Dog*, written shortly after Mann's political apologia "Reflections of an Unpolitical Man" and subtitled *An Idyll*, has been read as a retreat from politics into the pastoral world of domestic fiction.[35] In its intimate attention to the trials and tribulations of living with a dog—accepting him as part of the family, learning how to respond to his needs and to respect and care for him in sickness and in health—the novella should be seen rather, I would argue, as a protopolitics and examination of the intimate relations that make us who we are. To be sure, it is something of a domestic comedy in which husband and wife are replaced by human and canine (children appear in the background but have no important role) and in which, as in the "remarriage comedies" discussed by Cavell,[36] the man is disabused of his idea of the partnership he thought he wanted to secure. As the narrator is brought to see his inability to be a real "master" to his dog, Baushan, without compromising his status as gentleman (both master and gentleman are implied in the "Herr" of the title), he also comes to acknowledge the deep interdependence of his own and his dog's separate but shared worlds. It is Baushan, moreover, who is the agent of this acknowledgment by revealing, for instance, in a yawn that he has, as Derrida would say, "his own point of view."[37] " 'A fine master I have,' this yawn seems to say" (249). Unlike Tobias's one-sided dependency on Esau, the relation between the narrator and Baushan arises from and enables a "nobility" of the dog, if not of the "master"—a nobility that is not related to blood or birth.

The fact that Baushan is a male dog might invite us to read the story as an allegory of a homosexual romance or at least of alternative masculinities. Baushan, to be sure, is a creature whose expression of "carefully considered common sense" is said not to conceal (as bourgeois morality might have it), but to "affirm the masculinity of his life ethos, which his body in turn manifests physically" (222). Although the story is about a struggle between the forces of bourgeois morality and those of the untamed, "animal" body, Baushan is not only a metaphor for a healthy homoerotic gaze, but a dog whose particular dogness is fully present—a dogness whose place in society the narrator will have to evaluate. Indeed, the red-colored Baushan can be read as a stand-in for a male lover (reminding us of Gustav von Aschenbach's redheaded alter egos in Mann's *Death in Venice*) or for Esau, Tobias Mindernickel's reddish brown game dog.[38] Baushan offers Mann the opportunity to make good on the representation of society's abject relations—whether with pets or with men—that had been the site of such violence in that earlier story. More than a domestic fiction, furthermore, *Man and Dog* is a story of domestication, of "what domestication can be" (as Donna Haraway might say). For Mann, it is a comparison of two kinds of domestication: that of the Herr and what he may gain or lose through obedience to the laws of bourgeois society—laws he might be said to give himself—and that of the dog and what he both gains and loses through his own obedience to a master.[39] These domestications are not equal, to be sure, nor are the "freedoms" gained by domestication, but this overarching hierarchy should not blind us to the inequalities that weigh on both sides or to the importance for both man and dog of what they share as a couple.

Baushan, the reader learns from the start, is a very different dog than Esau. Both, moreover, are different from Perceval, the narrator's previous family dog, leading us to question whether, as Baushan's "master" suggests, the imprint of species weighs more than that of individual character or even experience. Unlike Esau, Baushan does not accept the metaphorical exchange of lentils for birthright and refuses his first meal, preferring to escape from his new owners and find his way back to his original home. Indeed, mastery on the part of the unnamed narrator cannot be bought; it must be earned through attention or what might even be called "attunement" to Baushan's particularity. Vicki Hearne writes of the importance of "reading" a dog rather than inferring temperament or behavior from some characteristic such as breed. Baushan, we are told, is a German short-haired pointer, but "if one goes by the book, Baushan isn't really a pointer at all" (220). To read him—which is to say, to know him—one must ignore those classifications of birth, breeding, and convention and acknowledge that which, according to the narrator, defies logic as well. "Both the hunter and the game dog predominate in Baushan, and this, if you ask me, qualifies him as a pointer, even if he doesn't owe his existence to some act of snobbish incest. That may well be the gist of the otherwise so confusing, logically disjointed words I address to him while I pat his shoulder" (222).

"It is the willingness to obey that confers the right to command," writes Hearne,[40] and in Baushan's case obedience is offered only to commands that respect his own "nature" or "character." Thus, Baushan refuses to perform mere tricks or to overcome obstacles that are not genuine, such as an outstretched pole that can more easily be run under or around as jumped over. And unlike Tobias, the Herr understands: to ask Baushan to jump it, he says "would be tantamount to a beating, for to demand something incomprehensible and—in its incomprehensibility—impossible from him is the same in his eyes as to seek pretense for a conflict, a disruption of friendship, a thrashing. . . . This is Baushan's perspective, as far as I can tell" (245). The last statement is significant, moreover, because it indicates a skepticism on the narrator's part that is an acknowledgment of his own limitations in understanding this dog whose actions are sometimes "utterly inscrutable" (245). It is an acknowledgment that Baushan has his own "logic" even if it is one that "language cannot adequately express" (245).

This separation of minds, however, does not prevent a profound relationship and even a mutual but healthy dependency from growing between the two. The narrator first describes this dependency from Baushan's point of view as a kind of "mitsein," or "being with," that occurs even in absence, even when there is a forced separation for long periods of time. "He is not at my side, at my command, but that in itself is the execution of a command, a negative form of being-at-my-side, so that there can be no talk of Baushan's leading an autonomous existence when we are apart" (235). Such a statement seems as much a projection onto Baushan of the narrator's own inability to shake the dog from his mind as it is of Baushan's dependence on him. He watches the dog through the glass door meant to separate them and feels the "sting" of leaving him at home on his trips into town. The intensity with which Baushan affects the narrator is made evident even in the narrative form itself, specifically in the number of "digressions" (287) he had no intention of including and in which he describes in detail various incidents of their life together. Indeed, these digressions are evidence of the narrator's inability to forget the dog, even as they describe events he would most like to forget—and from which Baushan recovers only by forgetting.

One of these "stories" the narrator "never intended to tell" (287) describes Baushan's extended stay at a veterinary clinic after revealing "unclean" symptoms—a bloody discharge from the nose—that do not go away. Evidence of his master's concern, the episode also reveals his avoidance, if not abjection of Baushan's animality, the need to separate himself from those natural elements of feces or blood or milk that are seen to defile the self and that are associated with the maternal–feminine.[41] We see this need at the beginning of the novella as the narrator and his family form a circle around Baushan to shield him (and themselves) from the embarrassment of onlookers as he "suffered" through bouts of diarrhea. With regard to the clinic story, the narrator is proud of his decision to take his dog to such an esteemed institution of science and suggests Baushan should also be proud to be the object of "such educated, exact, scrutiny" (281). But Baushan is "broken in body and soul" (286) from this esteemed and civilized treatment—broken, moreover, not only because of his neglected animality, but in a manner that reveals what is "human" in that animality without the gloss of metaphor behind which we hide our own emotional states. Animals, the narrator explains, are "less inhibited, more primal, thus in a sense more human about the physical expression of their emotional states than we are. . . . Baushan 'went,' to use such a phrase, 'with his head down'—that is he actually hung his head for all to see" (286). In other words, language, like the rational science of veterinary medicine, offers a means for us to avoid our own animal bodies, if not to appropriate animals for knowledge that yields no conclusion. The cause and origin of Baushan's bleeding is never found. What the narrator learns, however, is that his own health deteriorates in Baushan's absence. "As my own condition noticeably began to resemble Baushan's in his cage I concluded that the bonds of sympathetic affinity were more conducive to my well-being than the egocentric freedom for which I had longed" (285).

Sickness is a theme running through much of Mann's work, but, unlike *Death in Venice* or *The Magic Mountain*, *Man and Dog* does not simply associate health with bourgeois self-restraint and mastery or oppose health to the sickly attraction of decadent passion. To put it in the Nietzschean terms that Mann draws upon, the Apollonian ideal of individual freedom through self-mastery is not simply opposed to the Dionysian world of an erotic loss of self. Both of these paths can offer escapes from the responsibilities of emotional attachment as both refuse to see that illness may be a challenge to life and not opposed to it or that the self may be healthy in attachment to another. This is one of the lessons by which Baushan contributes to his master's "bildung"—indeed, by which Baushan brings him to change his understanding of what it means to be a master. But it is not the only lesson. As we are told that the clinic story passed and faded into oblivion—at least for Baushan—the narrator returns to the story he had meant to tell, a story not of his separation from the dog through language and learning, but of their joint passion—the hunt.

The episode of the hunt begins with an alternate ideal of human and, indeed, masculine potential, an ideal of authenticity exemplified not by the professor of medicine, but by the warrior: "How handsome he becomes! How idealized, how perfect! Thus the young hayseed from the highlands becomes perfect and exemplary. Thus the Alpine deer hunter comes into his own. Everything fine, authentic and superlative in him rises to the surface during these hunting hours and is displayed in all its glory. He's no pinscher, he's a game dog and speaks from everyone of the masculine and primal warrior poses he strikes in rapid succession" (278–279).

Baushan as hunter exemplifies that virile, animal instinct celebrated by Nietzsche and later by National Socialism, but he is separated from the Nazi's identification of this instinct with purity of breeding or race.[42] It is in the hunt, moreover, that the narrator's "gentlemanly sensibilities" rub up against his own animal instincts. On one level, hunting is what reveals a likeness in "hunter and dog." Both hold a certain disdain for the "bourgeois complacency" of the ducks, who "refuse to play along with the hunt" (296). Both have a certain amount of "good judgment asserting itself over passion" and stopping them from a "plunge into the river swells" (294). But where Baushan pursues his "womanly" prey to the final end of bone-crunching consumption, for the narrator the hunt is primarily a form of aesthetic play, and he takes pleasure in spectatorship, not in the hunt itself. At times, he admits to taking enjoyment in "imaginative" identification with the various participants. Unable to assist Baushan in the actual kill, however, he admits to a "guilty conscience" at "not being the man to 'drop' the hare like a real master" (291). Indeed, his identification with the unrestrained animal desires he admires is checked by the sympathy he feels for the helpless prey—as when a little "demon" of a hare jumps unaccountably into his arms: "I felt, or thought I could feel, its frantic little heart trembling. . . . This same creature was now huddled against me in its moment of greatest need and despair, clinging to my knees, clinging to the needs of the man who was not only Baushan's master but the master of the hare as well, i.e. its own master as much as Baushan's" (292). [43] Returning to the master/slave dialectic that defeated Tobias Mindernickel, Mann questions anew the status of mastery as the narrator is brought to weigh his responsibility to the hare and to Baushan—a "real" hunter. In the narrator's mind, a real hunter would simply and skillfully kill—like the "rough" man ("Mann" not "Herr") in overalls who, to the shame of the narrator and Baushan, appears out of nowhere to shoot a duck in midair with his rifle, leap into the currents that neither Baushan nor the narrator would brave, and take his kill.

This hunt scene and the appearance of this other man brings to memory the opposing and, indeed, antagonistic forces that divide and thereby confuse the narrator's sense of himself as master or "herr." "Civilization and Culture: an antagonism," wrote Nietzsche.[44] That antagonism structures the novella from the beginning: it opposes the two directions the narrator follows for his outings—whether into town on the train or into the woods with Baushan; it opposes the two dogs owned by the narrator, Perceval and Baushan, where the former is described as an "overbred eccentric" and the latter as having an "earthy common sense" (242); and it opposes the space of the clinic, where the body is repressed and denied, to the space of the hunt, where bodily passion is cultivated and gratified. Baushan's hunting instinct is like the "spell" that comes over him in the presence of another dog, where "both are bound to each other in some obscure, volatile relationship they are not allowed to deny" (248). As the dogs sniff each other's "procreative privates" and rub their bodies in an erotic if potentially threatening manner, the narrator acknowledges his foreignness to his dog's world as well as his impotence before these beasts who appear able to put embarrassment or shame behind them.

Nietzsche, of course, had as much contempt for shame as for pity—both attitudes from which humans needed to liberate themselves in order to fulfill their full potential. But to the extent that Mann's narrator may admire the dogs' ability to forget the "embarrassment" he witnesses, he also comes to see that shame not only may be a form of taming but may also preserve or give life. Just as the question of mastery arises from within the hunting ground, so the morality of culture, or of what might be called "animal life" over and against bourgeois civilization, is itself divided between the demands of the dog and those of the hare, which is to say between a domesticated life force that longs to free itself of discipline by giving into violence and the wild prey that longs to live. In siding with the hare rather than with Baushan or the hunter, the narrator gives the gift of (animal) life but offers it through a denial of the (animal) passion of the hunt. In this way, the Herr's examined civility (that is, aspiration rather than reflex) is what distinguishes him from Tobias, for whom culture and civilization are mutually destructive and for whom life affirmation depends on the domination and ultimate destruction of life. The question that then arises for the narrator and the reader is whether there is not some form or degree of civilization or domestication (and perhaps with it shame and pity) that is necessary for maintaining life.

In her study of Nietzsche's animal philosophy, Vanessa Lemm describes the antagonism of culture and civilization in relation to animality and memory: "Whereas culture is the memory of animality and the affirming and holding onto the human beings' continuity with the animals, civilization coincides with the forgetting of animality, the silencing of the animal within the human."[45] In Lemm's account, Nietzsche associates a healthy form of memory with culture and animality, in contrast to the burdensome past that humans carry

with them to safeguard a specific morality. Both culture and civilization, moreover, function through a form of forgetting. Civilization, as
described especially in the *Genealogy of Morals*, "tames" and thereby
forgets the human animal through an imposition of moral and legal
norms said to be necessary for life in society. This was Jacob's rule
over Esau, one that Mann's Tobias never attains in his attempt to rule
his own Esau. Culture, as Mann's later narrator comes to understand
though Baushan, offers a critique of civilization's specific forgetting not
in terms of some romantic dissolution of the self into nature, but rather
through a feeding of animal appetite and the forgetting of those mem-
ories that forestall future action. Man "wonders also about himself—
that he cannot learn to forget, but hangs on the past: however: far or
fast he runs, that chain runs with him," Nietzsche writes. Then man
says, "'I remember . . . ,' and envies the beast that forgets at once and
sees every moment really die, sink into night and mist, extinguished
forever."[46] Culture thus cultivates the "happy life" of the beast who
lives "unhistorically," knowing that "life in any true sense is absolutely
impossible without forgetfulness."[47] What Nietzsche calls the "historical sense," much like the "bad conscience" that results from the moral
life, "injures and ultimately destroys the living thing."[48]Although
Mann's story is critical of the repression of animality (and thus of animal forgetting), it also suggests that the cultivation of animality may
necessitate some degree of civilization and thus of memory, some
form of domestication as moral self-restraint so as not to give into
the death drives of culture (and perhaps the German militarism set
loose to support it). A civil domesticity—for Mann, one that fosters
the kind of domestic relation exemplified by the Herr and his *Hund*
(in contrast to Tobias and Esau), which is to say a relation engen-
dered by both empathy and responsibility—depends on a degree of
animal forgetting, to be sure. Referring to the hunting incident, the
narrator writes, "Time and forgetting have covered it over, and our
lives go on atop their swampy ground, which is the ground of all life"
(302). Or at least the narrator imagines he witnesses such forgetting
in Baushan as the dog slowly "regains his enthusiasm" for the hunt.
For himself, however, forgetting is not so easy or not just a matter of
time. Forgetting takes work; the narrator achieves it through writing. Writing for Mann is like "true" history for Nietzsche—a process

of working through memory, of relieving oneself of its burden.[49] As much as the narrator might like to enter Baushan's life or know how to enjoy his happiness, such truth is never delivered to him. Baushan, like Nietzsche's beast, responds only in a silent look that leaves both wondering "What am I, Who am I, Is that me?" (299).[50] Writing cannot answer those questions, but it can help by offering to those who ask the "promise" of a future relationship.[51] Writing, sustained as it is both by the self-mastery needed for solitary work and by the remembering to forget oneself so as to be moved by an animal and respond to his or her needs, is what allows the narrator to forget portions of the past for the sake of a future life to come. "Til tomorrow, Baushan," the narrator tells him in closing, "assuming I don't have to go out into the world" (302).

5

· ·

DOG LOVE/W(O)OLF LOVE

Writing Sex/Gender/Species

If *Man and Dog* is a domestic comedy (and a novel of domestication) from the man/master's point of view, Virginia Woolf's account of the relation between Elizabeth Barrett Browning and her dog, *Flush*, offers a domestic tale from the canine's point of view. Both works cast a critical eye on the structures of domestication through which human as well as animal identities are produced. Both, moreover, look quizzically at the affective attachment that domestication can create to bind mastered and master alike. In Mann's story, this affection troubles the Herr's sense of his own *Herrshaft*, or mastery, and the manliness on which it appears to rely. In Woolf's story, love between dog and mistress affords the latter a new source of strength and authority that ultimately translates to newfound freedoms for her and her dog. What I call "dog love" (borrowing the term from Marjorie Garber)[1] in *Flush* is paradoxically a bond that frees not only because of the perspective it offers on domesticity and the roles to which dog and mistress are confined, but also because it reveals, even as it acts to change, the patriarchal foundations that link domestic or private and public worlds. Written in 1933, five years after *A Room of One's Own* and five years before *Three Guineas*, *Flush* marks a transition from the aesthetic and economic feminism of the former work to the tougher, political feminism of the latter. "Too slight and too serious,"[2] Woolf wrote in her diary of this book that rehearses, in almost fairy-tale form, the observations she will make in *Three Guineas* regarding the "infantile fixations" of fathers who demand the sacrifice of their daughters. "It was the woman, the human being whose sex made it her sacred duty to sacrifice herself to the father, whom Charlotte Bronte and Elizabeth Barrett had to kill," she wrote in 1938; the "tyrannies and servilities" of the private world are the "tyrannies and servilities" of the public world, and if women are fettered to the domestic realm and not allowed to participate freely in the public, wars will never end.[3]

Flush sets up parallels between dogs' and women's domestic situations, but without claiming sameness between the two worlds. Indeed, it tries to investigate a dog's particular perspective and to represent the world from that perspective. Written as the biography of Elizabeth Barrett Browning's King Charles Spaniel and begun partially as a joke on the biographical style of her friend Lytton Strachey, *Flush* confronts head on the role of anthropomorphism in understanding and representing animals.[4] Although critics have found fault with the spaniel's humanlike features, I argue that Woolf's anthropomorphism is a deliberate strategy, the flip side of a zoomorphism that, according to Kate Flint, was visible in Woolf's "constant habit" of finding "animal correspondences" for her friends and acquaintances: Vanessa was a sheepdog, Leonard a mongoose, and so on.[5] Anthropomorphism can be compared to what, in feminist studies, has been called the problem of "saming" or seeing likeness where others have seen difference. Saming, as Naomi Schor explains, is to be contrasted with the mechanisms of othering exposed by Simone de Beauvoir whereby women were denied the intelligence, rationality, and full subjectivity of men and denied consequently the status of historical beings.[6] Almost thirty years after de Beauvoir, French feminist Luce Irigaray exposed the mechanisms of "saming" by which women are refused their difference— a difference, moreover, that cannot be defined simply in terms of a comparison or contrast with men. Saming is like anthropomorphism in that both reduce or disallow difference, whether differences between women and men or differences between nonhuman animals and humans. Like saming, however, anthropomorphism also acts as a corrective to what Frans de Waal has called "anthropodenial," a process that refuses to acknowledge the ways that nonhuman and human animals (or men and women) are alike, the ways certain so-called human characteristics are also characteristic of some nonhumans.[7] In Woolf, the practices of anthropomorphism and zoomorphism work to dislodge the reader and author from an objective standpoint from which to judge what is exclusively human or animal. The focus is instead on what is shared by domestic animals (human and non-human) as creatures—"Dearest Creature" was how Woolf addressed her friend and lover Vita Sackville-West—whose desires or longings for attachment and affection take shape within social structures that precede them.[8]

The importance of acknowledging anthropomorphism and, for that matter, zoomorphism as strategies is to underscore not only the degree of invention involved in writing any life, but also and more important the limitations of the *Umwelt* or world in which our writing takes place and that we may not be able to escape other than by refuting our own situatedness within history. As French philosopher Elizabeth de Fontenay writes, "It can help the friends of animals to understand that we cannot entirely purge ourselves of anthropocentrism except by taking ourselves for the God of Leibniz who is capable of seeing from all possible perspectives. This egoist, or even speciesist point of view (if one accepts the term) . . . is the effect of our finitude before being the mark of our power."[9] Woolf questioned what she saw as the role and authority of the Ego in writing by men and the way their particular point of view asserts itself as universal. In *A Room of One's Own*, she discusses the writing of "Mr A"—a random example chosen from a long patriarchal tradition of literature—which she admits to enjoying for its directness, evidence of a "freedom of mind" and "confidence . . . which had never been thwarted or opposed." But she eventually grows tired of it. "A shadow seemed to lie across the page . . . a shadow shaped something like the letter 'I,' a shadow that made it difficult to distinguish any other creature or reality; trees and women were equally 'shapeless in its mist.'"[10]

Like much of Woolf's own writing, *Flush* takes on the task of giving shape to other "creatures" and "realities" outside the self, all the while acknowledging that the representations of such "realities" are also shaped by one's own particular perspective. But the antidote to the authoritarian, overpowering, and patriarchal "I" (who will reappear in *Flush* in the dark, imposing figure of Mr. Barrett, who appears to speak with the "voice of God")[11] is not and cannot be an egoless or even sexless writing, she explains. Speaking to women in particular, she writes that they must write as women, but as women who are not conscious of their sex. "It is fatal for any one who writes to think of their sex. It is fatal to be a man or woman pure and simple."[12] Five years later in *Flush*, Woolf seems to suggest that it can also be "fatal" to write with the restricted consciousness of one's species. Indeed, already in *A Room of One's Own* she advises that one way to move outside the obstructions of self and sex consciousness is to see oneself in relation to the more-than-human world: "to escape a little from the common sitting-room and see human beings not always in their relation to each other but in relation to reality; and the sky, too, and the trees or whatever it may be in themselves."[13]

Woolf had first attempted such an escape in the make-believe biography *Orlando* (published shortly before *A Room of One's Own*), in which a male protagonist born during the Elizabethan era comes of age over a period of three centuries to awaken as a woman writer under Queen Victoria (though one whose sex is not ascertained until the twentieth century). In Orlando's virtual transcendence of sex and time, Woolf sought to understand more clearly the constraints they place on our lives and our writing. *Flush* adds to this effort by seeking to understand how such constraints are compounded by our so-called humanity and how they blind us to "other realities" that lie in the shadows. The project of *Flush* is to transcend the boundaries of human perception in order to evoke the social world as it may be perceived by a dog—through smell instead of sight and in meanings that cannot rely on the lexical for translation. The connections between *Orlando* and *Flush* thus reach beyond their status as mock biographies. Written as respites from the more difficult works *To the Lighthouse* and *The Waves*, respectively, and focusing on the historical and material conventions of culture that shape our lives and our consciousness, these biographies also search for an androgynous and mongrelized reality outside the cultural conventions that restrict what we know of such creatures as women and dogs and what we allow them to be.

Orlando and *Flush* thus go around the authority of the imposing "I" to search in the shadows for truths found not in conventional designations of identity, but in a kind of love. Held by his mistress before a mirror, Flush rejects the (mis)recognitions of the mirror stage and of a selfhood defined visually by others. "Was not the little brown dog opposite himself? But what is 'oneself'? Is it the thing people see? Or is it the thing one is? So Flush pondered the question too, and unable to solve the problem of reality, pressed closer to Miss Barrett and kissed her 'expressively.' *That* was real at any rate" (32).

Dog love thus pits the "real" body language of affection against the often unreal signs of identity that otherwise structure human relations and human–animal relations alike. The openings of *Orlando* and *Flush* are similar in their simultaneous invocation and critique of the conventions by which identities are established and hierarchized. Whereas the first line of *Orlando* addresses the "fashion of the time" that both reveals and disguises sex,[14] the first chapter of *Flush* calls attention to the fashion in dog breeds and the rules for eyes, muzzle, and skull by which a dog may or may not be accepted into the "Spaniel Club." "Light eyes, for example, are undesirable; curled ears are still worse; to be born with a light nose or a topknot is nothing less than fatal" (7). And "fatal" is hardly an exaggeration because only dogs exhibiting the cherished points will be allowed to breed. Thus, where gender designation in *Orlando* is seen to structure and limit the kinds of affective relations Orlando is permitted, in *Flush* pedigree similarly structures canine lives; indeed, it does so to an even greater extent because it determines whether a dog's sexual instincts will be gratified or denied altogether. What thus begins in both as an ironic gaze upon the marketplace of fashion ends with an exposure of the way convention, if not fashion, authorizes desire. Writing against such conventions in *Flush*, as in *Orlando*, Woolf conceives of a love that does not rely on fashionable or conventional identities or on permission from authority. Such is the "realness" of dog love. Because dogs and pets are considered of the family even as they are outside the species, pet love, Mark Shell explains, combines even as it transcends and traduces two practices that are normally taboo, bestiality and kinship, turning each into potentially chaste forms of affection.[15] If Elizabeth Barrett's love for Flush is anthropomorphic, moreover, it is so in a way that ultimately links humans to animals and to gods such that the bestial and the spiritual, the forbidden and the conventional, cannot be distinguished.[16] Daydreaming of a "hairy head pressed against her," Elizabeth asks herself, "Was it Flush, or was it Pan? . . . And did the bearded god himself press his lips to hers? For a moment she was transformed: she was a nymph and Flush was Pan" (27).

The first meeting of Elizabeth and Flush recalls the Platonic figure of love as the androgynous and narcissistic union of two opposed halves, one male and one female, each searching to complete him/herself in the other. Here, however, recognition of self in other takes place between male canine and female woman: "Each was surprised. Heavy curls hung down on either side of Miss Barrett's face; large bright eyes shone out; a large mouth smiled. Heavy ears hung down on either side of Flush's face; his eyes, too, were large and bright: his mouth was wide. There was a likeness between them. As they gazed at each other each felt: Here am I—and then each felt: But how different! Hers was the pale worn face of an invalid, cut off from air, light, freedom. His was the warm ruddy face of a young animal; instinct with health and energy" (18). The overlay of species difference onto gender difference works, however, to rewrite age-old descriptions of love as the completion of self or what Lacan, drawing on Plato, describes as an effort to restore the original wholeness lost or "lacking" as a result of sexual division—a "fusion making one out of two."[17] Such a union, as I have argued elsewhere, is more properly described as the destruction or appropriation of the other to the one.[18] Here, instead, uniting takes place imperfectly across the acknowledgment of unbridgeable difference. "Broken asunder, yet made in the same mould could it be that each completed what was dormant in the other? She might have been—all that—and he—But no. Between them lay the widest gulf that can separate one being from another. She spoke, He was dumb. She was woman; he was dog. Thus closely united, thus immensely divided, they gazed at each other" (18–19).

Dog love in *Flush* is thus described against this notion of completion in order to begin to imagine a form of desire/need that allows both likeness and difference to evolve. The two are alike in aspects of their appearance, in their common bright-eyed openness, yet separated by "the widest gulf," and this initial, reciprocal gaze signals the limits of love founded on narcissistic or, by extension, anthropomorphic projection (something neither Elizabeth nor the biographer can wholly escape) and the importance of acknowledging that the other will never be totally accessible to one's knowledge. For Woolf, moreover, the fact that in this instance speech cannot compensate for what the gaze cannot secure only increases the possibility for intimacy, albeit a "peculiar" one because it cannot rely on a shared language. "The fact was that they could not communicate with words, and it was a fact that undoubtedly led to much misunderstanding. Yet did it not lead also to a peculiar intimacy? 'Writing,'—Miss Barrett once exclaimed after a morning's toil, 'writing, writing . . . ' After all, she may have thought, do words say everything? Can words say anything? Do not words destroy the symbol that lies behind the reach of words? . . . But suppose Flush had been able to speak—would he not have said something sensible about the potato disease in Ireland?" (27, first ellipses in original).

Dog love takes place outside the kinds of comedies of Eros, where words mediate and compensate for a sexual relation that in Lacan's terms is consequently "impossible." To be dumb, in other words, is not to be lacking language, but to have an alternate means of apprehending the other and the world. Flush knows the world as "only the dumb know"—through sight, touch, and especially smell. "Not a single one of his myriad sensations ever submitted itself to the deformity of words" (87).

Civilization and the Dog's Discontents

That *Flush* avoids the comedies caused by words does not mean, however, that, as Woolf's narrator reminds her reader, a dog's life is "a Paradise where essences exist in their utmost purity. . . . Flush lived in no such paradise" (88). On the contrary, if Elizabeth is "prey to language," as Derrida might argue,[19] Flush, as property, is prey to his various owners' language and conventions. The relation between Flush and Elizabeth is from the start one of affinity across difference and across inequality. From the bedridden writer's perspective, Flush would offer what is inaccessible to her—knowledge of the world outside of words or, more simply, knowledge of the world outside, knowledge that comes from the ability to move freely through the world and consequently to follow one's own appetites and desires. But those masculine privileges are immediately taken from Flush upon entering Elizabeth's life and room. From Flush's point of view, life with Elizabeth is initially framed only in terms of loss—both his animal and his masculine freedoms are taken away: "Door after door shut in his face . . . they shut on freedom; on fields, on hares; on his adored, his venerated mistress" (17). In sum, the biographer writes, "all his natural instincts were thwarted and contradicted" (24).

Susan Squier was one of the first readers to underscore the similarities between Flush on his chain and Miss Barrett confined to her sofa—both restricted by patriarchal laws to a domestic world, both shaped by the poetry and philosophy of their masters as by the physical and institutional structures of their masters' lives.[20] But to the extent that *Flush* represents dogs and women alike as victimized creatures of their times, it also suggests that dogs and women can begin to change those structures and to shape, even as they are shaped by, the "spirit of the age." Indeed, the dog Flush is instrumental in this respect. Much as he was seen to inspire Elizabeth Barrett's poetry and as her accounts of that affection inspired Woolf to rewrite their love story, so does dog love become a civilizing force, but for a civilization that is not defined against or through the exclusion of animality and, by association, femininity. Although the attachment that grows between Flush and Elizabeth, in other words, might be seen as a symptom or product of domestication, an institution that confines women like animals, it also reminds us of those very social instincts that allowed for domestication to happen in the first place, the same instincts that allow Flush to "choose" his confinement with Elizabeth and to prefer the "thrilling tightness" of their bond to his freedom (25). Darwin attributes to these same instincts the very development of "moral qualities" we share with some animals: "These instincts are highly complex, and in the case of the lower animals give special tendencies towards certain definite actions; but the more important elements are love, and the distinct emotion of sympathy. Animals endowed with the social instincts take pleasure in one another's company, warn one another of danger, defend and aid one another in many ways."[21]

· · · · · · · · · · · · ·

Darwin's laudatory consideration of the social instincts is in stark contrast to the negative appraisal of animal instincts—understood as aggressive and divisive—evident from Thomas Hobbes to Freud. According to Freud, "The word civilization describes the whole sum of the achievements and regulations which distinguish our lives from those of our animal ancestors."[22] In *Civilization and Its Discontents*, first published in 1930, he cast the aggressive instincts as the greatest threat to civilization and consequently as what makes civilization necessary in order to protect individuals and communities from their animal or lupine nature.

> The element of truth behind all this, which people are so ready to disavow, is that men are not gentle creatures who want to be loved, and who at the most can defend themselves if they are attacked; they are, on the contrary, creatures among whose instinctual endowments is to be reckoned a powerful share of aggressiveness. As a result their neighbor is for them not only a potential helper or sexual object, but also someone who tempts them to satisfy their aggressiveness on him, to exploit his capacity for work without compensation, to use him sexually without his consent, to seize his possessions, to humiliate him, to cause pain, to torture and kill him. *Homo homini lupus.*[23]

Man is a wolf to man, Freud writes, accepting Hobbes's view of the state of nature. The only way man can protect himself against the dangers of nature is to submit those aggressive instincts to a greater rational authority and to the laws of civilization. Freud repeats the Kantian view that it is by means of such willed submission to law that man oxymoronically asserts his freedom and thereby distinguishes himself from animals. "Animals have a will," Kant wrote, but they do not have their own will, only the will of nature. "The freedom of humans is the condition under which the human being can be an end himself."[24]

Written three years after *Civilization and Its Discontents* was published, *Flush* offers a contrasting view to Freud by examining "civilization" from a dog's point of view (and through the dog from his mistress's point of view). Aggression is not what civilization protects against, but rather what it produces when Eros is restricted and when "natural" impulses of cooperation and sympathy are stifled. Woolf thus agrees with Freud's assertion that "people commonly use false standards of measurement . . . and that they underestimate what is of true value in life,"[25] but her work casts a critical eye on his statements concerning women and animals as necessarily the foes of civilization. The story of *Flush* demonstrates that it is rather because of women's commitment to Eros, defined in the unconventional form of a dog love that transcends the exclusive commitments of kin and kind, that they act as a counterforce to a civilization organized by the either/ or terms Freud describes: prey either to the aggressive instincts (the laws of animal nature) or to a dominating authority; either driven by the egoistic, sexual urges for love or having to repress those instincts in light of the political and social needs for community. *Flush* is a lighthearted but also serious consideration of how the pet–human relationship might contribute to the ongoing project of Enlightenment by contesting what we believe to be the human–animal divide and ultimately the anthropocentric opposition Freud sets up between satisfying so-called animal instincts and finding happiness.[26]

"If people like Flush choose to behave like dogs savagely, they must take the consequences indeed, as dogs usually do," Elizabeth Barrett writes to Robert Browning in Woolf's novel (47). If people are like Flush, then we may assume that Flush is like people who choose to be aggressive. Flush, indeed, suffers the consequences of giving in to his aggressive instincts early in Robert Browning's courtship of Elizabeth. A stranger to the Barrett household and one who slowly begins to take Flush's place by Miss Barrett's side and in her affection, Mr. Browning initially inflames Flush's jealousy. "The very sight of him, so well tailored, so tight, so muscular, screwing his yellow gloves in his hand, set his teeth on edge. He resolved to meet his enemy face to face and alone" (41). To Flush, Browning is the "neighbor" who, as Freud would say, is really more of an enemy, even though the Bible commands us to love that neighbor as oneself. "Why would we do it [love our neighbor], what good will it do us?" Freud asks, wondering especially how we are to achieve this when the neighbor "has more claim to my hostility and even my hatred."[27] For Freud, such an injunction is evidence of the inevitable conflict between egoistic and altruistic urges, between happiness and the demands of civilization, and between the exclusiveness of sexual love and the friendships formed through civilization. In Flush's case, however, this opposition turns out to be a false one. Flush comes to understand that a friend of his mistress must also be a friend of his. He thus learns to check or, more correctly, to sublimate his aggressive instincts and become for the reader an exemplar of moral freedom, which Kant (like Rousseau) explains is to be governed by a law one has freely chosen oneself.

> Twice Flush had done his utmost to kill his enemy; twice he had failed. And why had he failed, he asked himself? Because he loved Miss Barrett. Looking up at her from under his eyebrows as she lay, severe and silent on the sofa, he knew that he must love her forever. But things are not simple but complex. If he bit Mr. Browning, he bit her too. Hatred is not hatred, hatred is also love. Here Flush shook his ears in an agony of perplexity. He turned uneasily on the floor. Mr. Browning was Miss Barrett—Miss Barrett was Mr. Browning; love is hatred and hatred is love. (47)

In his demand for love, Flush undergoes "whirlpools of tumultuous emotions" and emerges to "survey a world created afresh" (47), a world where boundaries between sex and species as well as between hatred and love dissolve. Flush, in other words, sets the stage for the kinds of open relations that Bloomsbury was known for. To show his changed emotions for Mr. Browning, he offers to eat the cakes Mr. Browning had brought, not out of hunger—they were "bereft of any carnal seduction"—but out of a symbolic communion. "He would eat them now that they were stale, because they were offered by an enemy turned to friend, because they were symbols of hatred turned to love" (48).

It is perhaps more correct to say that, for Woolf, dog is "a wolf to man." Recent studies have shown that the aggressive, macho behavior that, for Freud, is such an integral part of the life of human males, is rare in canids and that canids may have "invented" that very "humaneness" that is considered to be the highest achievement of humanity.[28] Such "humaneness," according to ethologists, is what "makes it easy for wolfish families to form mixed, multi-species packs: humans, dogs, cats, goats, sheep, horses, living in harmony."[29] It may be Flush's wolfish ancestry that allows him to move from imaginary to symbolic not through renunciation or lack, but through an ever-widening acceptance of kinship across boundaries. Woolf, in other words, sees civilization and its animal origins in a manner that is less like Hobbes and more like Rousseau. Natural instincts may give rise to fear and distrust when an other is introduced, but as Flush's relations with Robert Browning and later with Robert and Elizabeth's baby demonstrate, aggressive instincts turn to accommodation as difference turns to likeness, and the enemy becomes an object of affection: "The baby was set on his back and Flush had to trot about with the baby pulling his ears. But he submitted with such grace, only turning round, when his ears were pulled 'to kiss the little bare, dimpled feet' that before three months had passed, this helpless, weak, puling, muling lump had somehow come to prefer him, 'on the whole,'—so Mrs. Browning said—to other people. And then, strangely enough, Flush found that he returned the baby's affection. Did they not share something in common—did not the baby resemble Flush in many ways?" (84).

Flush resembles the baby in that his desires and pleasures are not organized according to oedipal prohibitions and laws of kinship. Indeed, before the baby, Elizabeth's love of Flush empowers her to turn against those structures and institutions of domestication that are founded on abusive forms of domination and to stand up to her father's "civilization" in its refusal to recognize the value of love. This rebellion is most evident in the episode where Flush is stolen. Elizabeth understands that he is stolen because of a market system that turns dogs as well as "wives, slaves, horses, oxen, turkeys and geese" into commodities. Thus, Flush is thrown into the slums of Whitechapel together with a range of dogs, birds, bracelets, rings, and brooches. Whitechapel, as Squier has argued, is the underbelly Wimpole, opposed by class but linked not only by the economic dependence of each upon the other, but also by their masculine values:

> Although the battle lines at first seem drawn between Wimpole Street and Whitechapel, between the upper and lower classes, the confident generalizations of father, of brother, even of lover soon reveal the "class" whose interests such arguments really serve. Males have banded together against females and other marginal

creatures—against Barrett and Flush. Speaking as and for men, the various males in Elizabeth Barrett's life apply masculine logic to the problem of the kidnapping, ignoring both Flush's feelings in captivity and Barrett's own. The Whitechapel episode is a temptation scene; forced to choose between winning the approval of her male counterparts and saving Flush, Barrett is also being asked symbolically, to choose between two systems of morality—one masculine and impersonal, the other feminine and personal.[30]

That Elizabeth chooses the love of Flush over the "law and justice" espoused by her father and Mr. Browning is a watershed moment for her as perhaps also for her biographer. Elizabeth's statement "Think of Flush" is comparable to the momentous "Chloe liked Olivia" of *A Room of One's Own*, a statement about women's independence that initiates the bringing to light and to literature a realm of "underestimated" and unrepresented values. Having defied her father and lover with her refusal to sacrifice Flush for an abstract sense of justice, Elizabeth refuses to sacrifice her own love for her father's "law," eloping with Robert Browning and Flush to Italy, leaving "tyrants and dog stealers behind" (72). The Italy that Elizabeth and Flush discover, furthermore (far from the Italy of the 1930s),[31] is one where dogs and women are unfettered, free to roam and explore their hungers and desires. "He had no need of a chain in this new world; he had no need of protection . . . Fear was unknown in Florence; there were no dog-stealers here and, she may have sighed, there were no fathers" (77–78).

With *Flush*, Woolf thus begins to envision an alternative civilization to that of the fathers. Whereas Freud wrote that women represent all that is in "opposition" to civilization—family, sexual life, an incapacity for "instinctual sublimation"[32]—Woolf shows that even a dog can sublimate instincts and does so for family and for love, not in opposition to it. For Woolf, women and family life are not the obstacles to civilization, as Freud suggests, but harbor overlooked values that civilization needs to survive. The real threat to civilization is not women, but a male oedipal complex that turns women and other beings into coveted objects that can be exchanged or stolen and thus demands unwarranted restrictions upon their sexuality and their lives. "You are not fighting to gratify *my* 'sex instinct,'" Woolf writes to the imagined male recipient of her letter in *Three Guineas*, "nor to protect myself or my country." " 'For,' the outsider will say, 'in fact, as a woman, I have no country. As a woman I want no country. As a woman my country is the whole world.' "[33] Flush, too, breaks free of the bonds of nation and family in Florence to become "the friend of all the world." "All dogs were his brothers" (77). In Florence, Flush is able to experience "what men can never know—love pure, love simple, love entire; love that brings no train of care in its wake; that has no shame" (78–79). Liberated from his chain but still bound to Elizabeth by a "tie that was 'undeniably still binding,' " Flush has a life in Italy that redefines family because it offers an idealized image of the kind of love that humans have been denied to the detriment of civilization.

What the Nose Knows

Two years before writing *Civilization and Its Discontents*, Freud was presented with the first of a succession of chows who would accompany him through his later years in life. In that book, however, dogs appear only in a footnote, and there as the abject and shameful unrepressed of civilization. They reveal what humans left behind as they assumed an upright posture. In particular, dogs are held in contempt because they never evolved to repress either their sense of smell or their sexual instincts: "It would be incomprehensible, too, that man should use the name of his most faithful friend in the animal world—the dog—as a term of abuse if that creature had not incurred his contempt through two characteristics: that it is an animal whose dominant sense is that of smell and one which has no horror of excrement, and that it is not ashamed of its sexual functions."[34]

Dogs and smell, too, would take on very different meanings in later years and especially during the last year of Freud's life, however. That was the year he read and translated Marie Bonaparte's biography of her dog Topsy, a dog whose battle with cancer had parallels with Freud's own battle. On December 6, 1937, he wrote a letter to Bonaparte explaining his appreciation for the biography and, through it, for the love of animals: "It is, of course, not an analytic work, but the analysts' search for truth and knowledge can be perceived behind this creation. It really gives the real reasons for the remarkable fact that one can love an animal like Topsy (or my Jo-fi) so deeply: affection without any ambivalence, the simplicity of life free from the conflicts of civilization that are so hard to endure, the beauty of existence complete in itself. And in spite of the remoteness in organic development there is nevertheless a feeling of close relationship, of undeniably belonging together."[35]

Coming to regard dogs and dog love as something to be admired rather than to grow out of, Freud would also come to regard a dog's keen sense of smell as a capacity for truth telling rather than something to be ashamed of. Indeed, he would learn from his favorite chow something he would perhaps rather not have known. His cheekbone, gangrenous from cancer, produced such a stench that Lun reportedly shied away from Freud and crouched in the corner. If shame is really about "isolation from community," as Alice Kuzniar writes,[36] then it would appear that dogs and humans alike fear shame, as they also fear the smell of death as that which isolates absolutely. Lun was the instigator of Freud's shame, much as Derrida's cat provoked shame over his own exposed nakedness, his unclothed or unrepressed nature. "Shame is by nature recognition. I recognize that I am as the Other sees me," claimed Jean-Paul Sartre,[37] or, in this case, I recognize that I am as the other smells me. I am, in other words, a body that desires and that dies. Indeed, with smell, it is difficult if not impossible to disavow shame and project that unrepressed "nature" onto the dog or women. As Todd Dufresne writes, "Freud knew what that meant and looked at his pet with a tragic and knowing sadness."[38] Pace Heidegger and like Flush, Lun knew death and shared that knowledge with Freud—whether that knowledge meant the same thing to each or not. Heeding Lun's sign, Freud let his physician know that life was no longer worth living.[39]

Freud's ambivalence toward smell and toward dogs is to be contrasted with Woolf's embracing of smell in *Flush*, where it is viewed neither as something shameful nor as something to be repudiated, but rather as a foundation of civilization. "Yet it was in the world of smell that Flush mostly lived. Love was chiefly smell, form and colour were smell; music and architecture, law, politics and science were smell. To him religion was smell" (86). Smell is simply another means for reading and apprehending the world, a means that moves beyond the binaries of a civilization founded on shame. Whereas Freud hypothesizes that civilization evolved by the repression of smell, Woolf suggests that the need to repress results from the paucity of our human sense of smell, which, like our understanding of Eros, relies on binaries to describe what it doesn't know. "The greatest poets in the world have smelt nothing but roses on the one hand, and dung on the other. The infinite gradations that lie between are unrecorded" (86). The project of *Flush* is to begin to record those infinite gradations sensed by a world that must be sniffed in order to be recognized—a world, moreover, that is often hidden from sight. Such is the world of dog love, a world like that of "Chloe liked Olivia," which Woolf also described in *A Room of One's Own* as full of "half lights and profound shadows."[40] Just as the representation of women's lives had previously been circumscribed by "the capricious and colored light of the other sex," so the representation of dogs' lives and loves has been constrained by the blinding light of the "human," especially as defined through patriarchy. To peer into dog love is to redefine the nature of Eros as necessarily more than, if not other than the heterosexual, species-specific desire of a male for a female. It is a love of family that expands the boundaries of family, a love that binds without domination. Dog love, we might say, is polymorphously productive rather than polymorphously perverse and, as such, a force for a more just and contented civilization.

Part III

· ·

GRIEVING
ANIMALS

6

. . . .

A PROPER DEATH

Dying Like a Dog

"A dog should die like a dog," writes Richard Klein, "not cruelly, but with a respectful matter-of-factness, unaccompanied by the rituals of human mourning."[1] Writing against what he sees as a dangerous tendency in postindustrial society to humanize pets in such a way that we may be encouraged alternately to animalize humans, Klein would approve of the death of Woolf's Flush, which is striking in its simplicity, its matter-of-factness. Flush, apparently with knowledge of his impending death, suddenly rushes home "as if he were seeking refuge" and leaps onto the couch where his mistress is seated. Turning his eyes toward her face, they share one last exchange of looks before Elizabeth Barrett-Browning continues her reading. "Then she looked at Flush again. But he did not look at her. An extraordinary change had come over him. 'Flush' she cried. But he was silent. He had been alive; he was now dead. That was all. The drawing-room table, strangely, stood perfectly still."[2]

The stillness of the table, signaling the absence of those communicating spirits that populated Barrett's drawing room to make table legs move and give signs of life after death, signals also the finality of the dog's death. Is Woolf reminding her readers that dogs have no soul, or does the finality of Flush's death call attention to the shared mortality of all animals—human and nonhuman alike, in spite of the way such drawing-room practices might seek to hide it?

The end of Leo Tolstoy's short story "Strider: The Story of a Horse," written between 1883 and 1886, presents a similar contrast between human and animal death and the ceremonies surrounding each. Strider is the title character of the story and also its occasional first-person equine narrator—he tells the story of his life to the other barn horses while the humans are sleeping. Much like Anna Sewell's *Black Beauty*, Strider's story is that of a "noble" horse (despite being mocked as a piebald) who is overworked, exchanged from master to master, and abused in the name of property. After his death, Strider's body is left in a field, where, the other narrator tells us, it feeds a family of wolves—the mother wolf bites off and chews pieces of flesh that she then regurgitates for each of her five cubs. Months later a peasant finds the few remaining bones of Strider's body and puts them to use as well. Juxtaposed to this death that is both a return to nature and a recycling is the death of Strider's first master, Serpukhovskoy:

> Just as for the last twenty years his body that had walked the earth had been a great burden to everybody, so the putting away of that body was again an additional trouble to people. He had not been wanted by anybody for a long time and had only been a burden, yet the dead who bury their dead found it necessary to clothe that swollen body, which at once began to decompose, in a good uniform and good boots and put it into an expensive coffin with tassels at its four corners, and then to place that coffin in another coffin of lead, to take it to Moscow and there dig up some long buried human bones, and to hide in that particular spot this decomposing maggoty body in its new uniform and polished boots and cover it all up with earth.[3]

Humans, of course, are not the only animals who bury their dead. We know that elephants, for example, have elaborate grieving practices that include a form of burial and visits to gravesites. But, for Tolstoy, humans are the "dead who bury their dead." In death, as in life, we embalm our bodies with useless ornaments and so preserve them from serving others, from offering a gift of life in death. According to

Heidegger, humans are nevertheless said to be the only animals who "properly" die because only humans know of death "as such"—only humans live life with the knowledge of their finitude. "Mortals are they who can experience death as death. Animals cannot do this."[4] But such knowledge of death has little to do with funereal rituals that defy finitude in the attempt to hold onto life's property, if not life itself, even into death. The elaborate, jeweled casings over Serpukhovskoy's body suggest that even it must be preserved in its proper form, along with the property he accumulated while living. In contrast to his horse, Serpukhovskoy illustrates what French feminist Hélène Cixous describes as the masculine "realm of the proper" "set into play by man's classic fear of seeing himself expropriated . . . deprived." History itself, she writes, is a response to this fear: "Everything must return to the masculine."[5] For Tolstoy, it is not the feminine, but the animal who resists this economy of return to the masculine by giving without return. The very propriety, if not property, of mortals, he intimates, is what stands in the way of a life and death that can serve others, of what we might call an ethical death even if an improper one. Perhaps, then, for Tolstoy, a human should die like a dog or a horse, unaccompanied by rituals of mourning.

What, indeed, is a proper death for a dog or a human, and what, if anything, determines what are "proper" rituals of grief and mourning? I pursue these questions by examining a range of representations (and experiences) of animal death, beginning with the questions raised by Woolf and Tolstoy regarding the differences between human and animal death or between the deaths of pets and other animals and the kinds of mourning or grief that each may or may not allow for. These questions have become especially pronounced in the face of a current theoretical and aesthetic fascination with animal "becomings" or "becoming animal"—to use the term from Gilles Deleuze and Félix Guattari that, in my mind, leaves the question of death behind. As I argue, the fascination with becomings functions as a kind of melancholia that resists or even subverts practices of mourning, while categorizing "the animal" as the living dead.[6]

In his *Second Discourse*, Rousseau writes of the "knowledge of death and of its terrors" that humans acquired in their move away from the animal condition, "for an animal will never know what it is to die."[7] Nevertheless, the experience of loss is not foreign to animals. On the contrary, writing of "the mournful lowing of cattle entering a slaughter-house," Rousseau claims that animals deeply feel sentiments such as pity for the dead. Indeed, he argues, identification with "the suffering animal" was much stronger in the "state of nature," and humans lost their capacity for pity and empathy as they moved out of that state. Rousseau's emphasis on how we respond to the death of another rather than to the idea of death or to our own death (if that were possible) offers a different perspective about what it might mean to "die properly." Indeed, if his mention of the slaughterhouse seems less than arbitrary, so, too, the endings of *Flush* and "Strider" ask us to consider, on a first level, what constitutes a "proper" death and whether it is determined by the ontic cause or by the ontological relation to death. Few animals die of old age, as Flush does, while gazing into the eyes of a beloved. Strider's killing by a "knacker" comes closer to the manner in which most domestic animals die, even as their deaths may be regarded as "easing" the "burden" of their miserable lives.[8] Strider lives to an old age (something few "farm animals" today are allowed to do), which may be as much blessing as additional curse. Evidence of grief or identificatory suffering is strangely absent from both *Flush* and "Strider," where, moreover, the absence of ritual surrounding the horse's death is what allows for his body to offer life to others. Are we to understand this becoming meat for another as a form of ethical ecology rather than another instance of animal sacrifice, though for whom or in whose name it is not clear?

The question was brought home to me at the death of my "own" horse, the horse whose guardian I had been for close to fifteen years. *Guardian*, as I explained earlier, has become the preferred term for those who have and care for pets, but because horses are considered livestock rather than pets, it is really ownership (and money) that can make a difference in terms of how they die and what happens after their death. Cacahuète, "Peanut"—the nickname she earned from her rich, peanut butter color—stopped eating in her old age and was sickened from what appeared to be a lymphoma. After discussions with the vet, I decided that euthanasia was the best response, though not an easy one. It was made more difficult by the fact that at the moment I made my decision, I also had to make arrangements for her "remains."

If I did nothing, the renderer would come to pick up the body in the morning. Such an idea struck me as indecent. Cacahuète, I thought, deserved a better afterlife; she would not be turned into glue or, even the more likely, dog food—even if that might mean her life fed others. There was an alternative. The vet gave me the name of a woman who had recently begun a cremation service for horses (there are very few in the country); her mother had also opened the first equine cemetery in the area. When I called her, her first questions were about my horse—what she had been like, what she looked like, what I most missed about her. She seemed to know that I wanted this for my horse. In hindsight, I could be cynical about it—wondering if getting me to cry was a business ploy. But in hindsight I also realize that mourning means attesting to a life. We are not only autobiographical animals; we are biographical animals who seek to acknowledge those whose lives have been entangled with ours, whose lives have changed ours. *Ownership* may be the legal term with which we describe such relations, but on an emotional level the term does not describe our mutual dependence. I wanted such a testament to my horse's life, and I believed that such a testament depended on "proper" treatment of the body—one that did not grind it up to be sold on the market. What I wasn't prepared for was the cost of cremation or the realization that the high cost was due to the amount of time and energy it took to burn a horse's body. A dog's body can be cremated in a matter of minutes—a horse can take a day. I thought of the ecological effects, the toll on the environment. Is such a ritual of mourning selfish? I wondered. Is it worth it? For whose sake am I doing this? I thought, remembering Coetzee's character David Lurie in *Disgrace*, who asks the same question as he makes sure each euthanized dog in the animal clinic has a proper burial.

Melancholy Becomings

In Tolstoy's "Strider," what is especially disgraceful in the elaborate rituals surrounding Serpukhovskoy's death is that they appear to serve no one but Serpukhovskoy himself. They remind us of a self-serving life and deny the ultimate importance of mourning rituals for those who grieve or who want to remember, and they thus turn a potentially proper ritual into one of impropriety. Despite the fact that Flush and Strider are denied such rituals, their "biographies" stand as testaments to lives that have been lived and are worth remembering. They suggest, moreover, that a proper or successful mourning depends on the ability of the living to name and so to reconstruct the identity of the dead along with a place and moment of death. This link between mourning and naming may exist in spite of what Walter Benjamin sees as the unavoidable nature of human language to name imperfectly or to "over-name," considering that "things have no proper name except in God." "Over-naming," he adds, "is the deepest reason for all melancholy and (from the point of view of the thing) of all deliberate muteness."[9]

Much of recent art and theory has nevertheless come to focus on those places of linguistic imperfection—wrong naming, overnaming, or impossible naming—that stand as evidence of our deficiencies as humans, if not of the hubris of our presumed separation from nature even in the act of mourning it. Death has become that which we cannot name properly, that which defies our linguistic skills and creates disorder in our conceptual abilities. A recent video piece by the British-born artist Sam Taylor-Wood is a case in point. Beginning with an image of a dead animal, it proceeds to investigate the processes of life after death in the form of endless transformations of the body as it is eaten away by some sort of unidentifiable maggot or organism. Entitled *A Little Death* (2002), the video begins with an art historical reference to a still life in the style of the eighteenth-century French genre artist Jean-Siméon Chardin. A dead hare is nailed by one foot to a bare wall, its head and arms resting on a table beside one perfect peach. Like Bill Viola's video examined in chapter 2 and even more like Viola's later videos, this film, too, is a study of time and especially of the incremental moments between life and death, if not of life in death. Slowly, very slowly the still life begins to move and change under the invasive force of whatever it is that eats away at and turns the hare's dead body into dispersed traces of bodiless fur. What is most stunning, if not repulsive, is how, midway into the four-and-a-half-minute video, the force of those organisms appear to breathe life into the hare as they lift the body into the air, only for it to fall again to a second, "little death." An erotic reading of this video as a narrative of erection and detumescence is enforced by "little death" in the title—the translation of a French term for orgasm (*la petite mort*) or, more precisely according to French philosopher Georges Bataille, to the moment of loss after orgasm. The peach, by contrast, remains untouched, impervious to change, and a witty reminder of the ways art and technology can manipulate our perception of time and bodies.

More important, perhaps, is the way that Taylor-Wood forces her viewer to confront the collusion of death and the erotic, art and sadism, nourishment and violence, if not also the tragic and the comic. This is also the focus of Bataille's discussion of the *petite mort* in *The Tears of Eros*. There he describes a drawing from the caves of Lascaux where a man lies prostrate before a dying bison, his (the man's) penis "unjustifiably" erect. "We cannot imagine a more obscure contradiction," writes Bataille, "nor one better conceived to guarantee disorder in our thinking" than the "essential" and "paradoxical accord . . . between death and eroticism."[10] That this "complicity" of the tragic and the erotic should take place around the animal's death should not be surprising from Bataille's perspective, given his view of the advent of the human "out of the animal" and into a state that is conscious of death and eros alike.[11] If animality is the first state of unknowability because "nothing . . . is more closed to us than the animal life from which we are descended,"[12] eros and death constitute secondary states of which we are conscious (unlike animals), but whose arrival—whether in the moment of erection or in the moment of death—is inexplicable and unknowable. For Bataille, it is thus not only through consciousness of death that man is distinguished from animals, but also through the taking on of the erotic as a conscious project—perhaps in defiance of our lack of mastery over it. Unlike nonhuman animals, humans "calculate" pleasure and thereby substitute "play" for instinctive reaction.[13]

Taylor-Wood evokes this space that is outside or between "proper" distinctions between animal and environment, subject and object, and life and death through the dissolution of form into illegible shapes and shades of light. Death is visualized as Derridean "aporia"— "the crossing of a border . . . a trespassing . . . or . . . a transgression."[14] Her piece offers that experience of "visual intensity combined with conceptual instability" that Steve Baker understands to be characteristically postmodern.[15] Quoting Donna Haraway, Baker argues that postmodern art and philosophy share an enterprise for taking "pleasure in the confusion of boundaries, and for responsibility in their construction,"[16] although I would contest the extent to which "responsibility" is a postmodern trait. Taylor-Wood's postmodern aesthetic seems closer to Bataille's own aesthetics of transgressive "excess," not only in terms of a willed "disorder in thinking," but also in the way such aesthetics appear to sidestep (if not fly in the face of) ethical and political concerns. Not unlike in "Strider," where the horse's corpse becomes food for the wolves of the forest, in Taylor-Wood's video the hare becomes food (and life) for a host of maggots. But this representation of death as a gift of life has a very different status in the two works. Tolstoy's death scene is a moment in a work that otherwise seeks to reconstruct the "story of a horse." The ending contributes to this story by leaving us with a confusing combination of emotions—sorrow over Strider's death mixed with a hesitant joy over the way nature has reclaimed him—that makes us wonder about the rights and wrongs of the horse's death. In Taylor-Wood's video, death happens not in a moment, but over time, denying the moment of "perishing" that for Heidegger defines animal death. But neither is this "proper death" because it disregards and undoes the identities of character and plot set up by the initial still life.[17] Taylor-Wood mesmerizes her audience by focusing on the process of ingestion and incorporation that makes it impossible to know who or what is doing the eating or being eaten. Epistemological uncertainty takes precedence over any ethical concerns.[18]

That postmodern art has shown a distinct preference for such epistemological questions over ethical ones has led Steve Baker to asks specifically, "Can contemporary art address the killing of animals?" Baker suggests that the concern to "straightforwardly right wrongs may be hard to reconcile with postmodern art's fascination with a sense of the rightness of things gone wrong."[19] Dominick LaCapra has voiced a similar worry over the postmodern "fascination with excess" and its effect on historical practice. Speaking specifically to the concern for violence done to animals, LaCapra writes that "this concern becomes acute when violence is not only seen (however contestably) as useful or necessary to achieve certain results (a basic reform a transformed polity, a hoped-for experimentally discovered cure for a human disease even if it means doing violence to other animals) but is also transfigured in sacred, sublime, redemptive, or foundational terms."[20] LaCapra sees a danger in the attention that historians and literary critics are giving to a "post-secular" or "negative sublime" (and it is in such a category that I would include Taylor-Wood's video)—a sublime that is conceived within a paradigm of trauma because it exceeds our capacities for intelligible expression. This negative sublime "may well induce an evasion or misconstruction of specific historical, social and political problems, including the status and use of the animal in society."[21] It is significant, in this respect, that Taylor-Wood's *A Little Death* begins not with the actual killing of the hare—that event is obscured by the entrancing "little death"—but with its nailed, Christ-like body. Unlike Flush and Strider, whose (fictional) biographies stand as testaments to lives that impacted others,[22] the hare as well as the material manifestation of death and its lively undoing become objects of visual fascination, what might be called a "sublime livingness," that are ultimately detached from the dying animal.[23] "What's that on the wall?" we ask at the end, or "Why is the peach unchanged?" but not "What happened to the hare?"

LaCapra advocates a process of working through and mourning in order to retrace the events and move beyond such immersion in the blinding intensity of existential trauma. Both terms, *working through* and *mourning*, he takes from Freud, for whom mourning is understood to be a healthier response to trauma and loss than melancholia—a state characterized by an immersion in ambivalence and excess.[24] Indeed, despite the often liberatory and deliberately subversive nature of Baker's *The Postmodern Animal*, much of the animal art discussed in it can be called melancholic because of the way it resists the working through of mourning.[25] This is especially true of works associated with Deleuze and Guattari's notion of "becoming animal" that foreground the inadequacy or impossibility of assigning singular identity to "assemblages" that appear to exist between or beyond boundaries of species, gender, and even life and death.[26] Baker begins his article "What Does Becoming-Animal Look Like?" with Deleuze and Guattari's statement, "Either stop writing or write like a rat." A challenge to the writer and artist alike, this statement asks both to draw on the power of the animal pack in order to prolong "moments of upheaval" of the self. "Who has not known the violence of these animal sequences which uproot one from humanity, if only for an instant, making one scrape at one's bread like a rodent or giving one the yellow eyes of a feline? A fearsome involution calling us toward unheard-of-becomings," ask Deleuze and Guattari.[27] Becoming animal is about undoing identity, exploring the aporias or in-betweens of identity, presumably in order to challenge and even explode conservative, bourgeois expectations of who we may become in life, if not to contest what it might mean "to be" at all. But such melancholic "becoming" runs counter to the work of mourning, which cannot be accomplished except by making the kinds of distinctions and reconstructing the identities that "becoming animal" resists, if not undoes. As LaCapra writes, "Processes of working-through, including mourning and modes of critical thought and practice, involve the possibility of making variable, complex distinctions—not dichotomous binary oppositions—that are recognized as problematic but still function as limits, bases of judgment, and resistances to the blurring of distinctions."[28] Put simply, mourning depends on knowing who or what is lost.

The tension between the process of "becoming animal" as a melancholic undoing of identity and the work of mourning is at the center of Hélène Cixous's short story "Shared at Dawn," where, moreover, there are species becomings as well as gender becomings. It is a brief story of intense emotions inspired by the narrator's efforts to prevent her pet cat from coming into contact with a bird that has been trapped in the house. Told in retrospect, the story begins from the perspective of failed mourning (failed because there is no dead body) as the narrator recounts the aftermath of the two creatures' thwarted meeting:

> We search in vain for quiescence, my cat and I.
> The house is full of remnants, it emprisons us in its memory of sorrows—they are on the entryway carpet, on the floors, in the corners of the living room, in the kitchen right up to the sink; they stop there, then they start off again toward the balcony, and there, stuck for eternity between the eleventh and twelfth banister: miniscule, powerful claws caught in the little squares of lattice-work.[29]

As the title intimates, this story is about those moments described by Deleuze and Guattari when "something shared or indiscernible" is revealed among bird, cat, and woman and when boundaries are transgressed to produce "zone[s] of indetermination or uncertainty."[30] The instigator of such "becomings animal" are traces of life caught in the latticework—a what or who that turns into what Derrida has called the "absolute arrivant," the guest who annihilates "the very border that delineated a legitimate home."[31] Thought alternately to be a leaf and then a bird, dead and then alive, this creature "traps the narrator" herself with its "threatening strangeness" and throws her into a "state of irresolution" as she struggles with the idea of death in her home and a dead bird taunting her cat. The upheaval multiplies as the thing reveals itself to be a bird "on this side" of the lattice and not the other, alive and not dead. "Concerning the dead body, I have the feeling of being violently attacked. Everything is aiming at me: stability, solidity, the creature must have spent the night lying in wait for me, nothing could make it let go, not even a storm, and death gives it a monstrous force, stand up to us, knowing no time, no fatigue. What it inflicts on me is the strangeness of the other side. Faced with a dead creature, there's nothing we can do, Right?"[32]

What ensues is a series of events that throw all domesticated (and oedipalized) identities into question, revealing the fragility of the domestic and domesticating structures that try to keep such identities in their proper place and form. Finding only remnants of the bird, the cat is caught in "uncertain mourning" and retreats to her bed "in the form of a bird." The narrator herself, meanwhile, identifying with the cat's frustration, turns feline as she searches for the bird's "lukewarm body" so that she might "give it sharp little blows with [her] paw" and offer its body to the cat, whom she calls "my counterpart, my betrothed, my little bride."[33]

How are we to understand such identifications between species and genders and between grief and predation? In Cixous's story, I argue, "becomings" must be understood as manifestations of melancholia, where, as Freud explains, "the object has not perhaps actually died, but has become lost as an object of love" (or even of hunger) and where, despite the belief in loss, "one cannot see clearly what it is that has been lost."[34] Expounding on this state, Freud explains that identification with the lost object becomes a mode of preserving it within the self in an act that is central to ego formation. Building on Freud's theories, Judith Butler has linked such identification with a lost object to the means by which the ego assumes a gendered status. This is especially true, she argues, when that lost object has been prohibited as an object of love—such as for a homosexual attachment.[35] Gender must thus be understood as the effect of the arduous processes of assumed and refused identifications. Can we say the same about ourselves as a species—that our understanding of ourselves as human is a similar accomplishment achieved through a series of repudiated attachments or that we become human by growing out of our childhood identifications with other animals? In Cixous's story, both gender and species appear as sublimated identifications with a lost or abjected animal other—whether bird or cat—that has been internalized. The liberatory potential of "becoming" is thus connected to the melancholic's refusal (or inability) to subscribe to the law of sex or species, to erase boundaries between kin and kind, pet and lover, but also between love and violence, emulation and ingestion.

But if Cixous's narrative appears to respond to the Deleuzean call for the writer to prolong such instants of "becoming animal," it does so only by calling attention to the loss that accompanies such moments—a paradoxical loss of mourning. The narrator (if not also her cat), "emprisoned" in a state that she cannot move beyond, is stuck in a painful melancholia because what is lost to her is unknown and unavailable to representation. Insofar as this state entails a loss of bearings between life and death, it takes on a gendered character that links the cat's loss to a mother's loss and both losses to the narrator's lost identification as mother. "The cat's sorrow is that of a mother who can't find her baby in the house anymore," we are told, at which point the narrator questions her own status as mother. "I know that it's the mother who is supposed to struggle with death. And I couldn't, I can't." Unable to "touch" the "dead" animal and so clear death from her daughter's house, she asks herself, "Will I still be able to assert that I'm your mother?"[36]

Animal death and animal loss thus share something with the mother's loss and the loss of motherhood in Cixous's story, and although their connections are never explicit, I would like to pursue what appears to be their link to a loss that cannot be worked through by mourning.[37] Indeed, as Cixous and Luce Irigaray suggest elsewhere, the loss of the mother goes unmourned because it "radically escapes any representation."[38] Entry into the realm of the Symbolic—which is to say, into language—happens only through separation from the mother's body and thus through a loss of that which never was present to representation in the first place. This is why Cixous claims that women have a different relationship to mourning. "I believe women *do not mourn* and this is where their pain lies."[39] Elaborating also on the psychoanalytic background to women's melancholia, Butler writes: "As in the Lacanian perspective, for Abraham and Torok the repudiation of the maternal body is the condition of signification within the Symbolic. . . . In effect the loss of the maternal body as an object of love is understood to establish the empty space out of which words originate. But the refusal of this loss—melancholy—results in the failure to displace affect into words; indeed the place of the maternal body is established in the body, 'encrypted,' to use their term, and given permanent residence there as a dead and deadening part of the body."[40]

Cixous admittedly understands this lack of mourning as a sign that women do not need to hide over or compensate for what it is they may themselves have lost in the lost object—there is no need for those elaborate rituals described in Tolstoy. With regard to loss, a woman "lives it, gives it life," rather than putting it behind her or outside of her. In relation to loss, she is "neither outside nor in."[41] This neither/nor relation to loss is what produces the "uncertain mourning" of Cixous's narrator as well as the seductive violence of Taylor-Wood's video. Both are narratives or antinarratives that find it difficult to represent what is lost or loss itself, asking instead, "Who/what is it?" "Who/what am I?" and "What will I become without you/it?" These questions are unanswerable except as they reveal the fundamental and inescapable fact of our interdependence as living beings and hence our reciprocal implication in others' lives.[42]

Living loss in such a way that it becomes impossible to represent what has been lost has both personal and political risks. This is why Cixous and Irigaray's elaboration of a feminine melancholia is coupled with efforts to write, remember, and mourn the mother. In this way, they hope to call attention to and eventually change the repression of motherhood within patriarchal culture. And here lies the important link to the animal, over whose similarly abjected or sacrificed body the foundations of culture (as opposed to nature and hence "the animal") have also been constructed. To put it in the more blunt terms of the British Animal Studies Group, "Almost all areas of human life are at some point or other involved in or directly dependent on the killing of animals [. . .]. This killing is ubiquitous and omnipresent . . . largely invisible in the public domain."[43] And because the loss produced by this killing is invisible, because it too largely escapes representation, it also remains unmourned.

Powers of Mourning

Mourning, Butler has argued more recently, is not the "goal of politics," but "without the capacity to mourn we lose that keener sense of life we need in order to oppose violence."[44] Might mourning the dead animal also be a means of counteracting the silence that exists over its loss and a means to acknowledge and possibly work to change the ways that culture is also constructed over its dead body? There is, of course, no guarantee, but the very possibility should lead us to be wary of those "becomings animal" that imprison Cixous's narrator and of our own attraction to a melancholic or negative sublime that refutes distinctions between life and death as between human and animal. By foreclosing the reconstruction of identities on which a successful mourning depends—and thus what Butler calls a "grievable life"—these becomings may also foreclose the possibility that mourning be a resource for a political or ethical response or both.

"What makes for a grievable life?" Butler asks in *Precarious Life*, and how does grief consequently become a political issue? Written after the events of September 11, 2001, and concerned especially with persons and peoples who have been the targets of violence and military warfare even as their deaths are prohibited from "public grievability," Butler's book focuses on the ways that grief contributes to the norms by which "the human" is constituted and, alternatively, the ways that some are dehumanized by having their deaths unrecognized or unmourned. Violence against such targets doesn't count as violence because it leaves no mark or because, unacknowledged, it "leaves a mark that is no mark."[45] And how can one protest a violence that isn't seen as such? This question has particular valence for the animal killings that happen on a daily basis, deaths—whether in factory farms or oil spills—that are consequently calculated in economic terms, but not in terms of grief. Of course, for Butler, death of an animal is by definition not grievable—grief being reserved for and constitutive of what is human. As Chloe Taylor has also remarked, "Again and again [Butler] equates being a 'real life' or a 'grievable life' with being a human life."[46] Transferring Butler's reasoning to animals' situation, Taylor continues that it thus stands to reason that "if to be a real life is to be a human life, whereas to be inhuman—to be another species of animal, for instance—is to be 'already dead' and something which 'cannot, therefore be killed' then animal lives were never real and their deaths are not real either. Thus we can kill them with impunity—as we do—and make them suffer continually during their short lives—as we do—since those lives are not lives at all and no murder has, therefore, taken place."[47] Indeed, we do kill animals with impunity—this, Derrida reminds us, is one of the effects of the category of "the animal"—and with legal disregard for the pain we cause given that so-called "food animals," for example, are largely exempt from anticruelty laws.[48] The majority of domestic animals raised in factory farms or experimental cages or impounded in shelters are "not quite living," to be exact, and this definition may contribute to the fact that if there is much of a "discourse" at all concerning the lives and deaths of these animals, it is a "silent and melancholic one," in which, as Butler describes for certain dehumanized people, "there were no lives and no losses."[49]

My point is not to reopen questions of whether violence done to animals is the same as violence done to peoples (it may be analogous without being the same, as Marjorie Garber has argued)[50] or even to set up a scale of comparison. Rather, I want to emphasize how not only with regard to matters of killing but also with regard to matters of grief, nonhuman animals belong to *the constitutive outside of the human*, designating the boundary between what or who is and is not grievable according to what or who is or is not humanized. As evidenced by the dehumanizing prohibition of public mourning for some peoples and the ever-expanding grief industry for pets (including cemeteries, support groups, and interfaith blessings to ensure the protection of their souls after death), a proper death is clearly refused to some humans but granted to some nonhuman animals. Indeed, if grief is foreclosed to Taylor-Wood's hare, unlike to Flush or Strider, this is also because of its status as a nonindividuated, undomesticated animal who belongs with the pack (as Deleuze and Guattari would say) rather than with the humanized world of pets. It has the status of the bird in Cixous's story, but also of the many animals in factory farms whose undistinguished deaths we are not meant to witness and to which we are unsure how to respond.

The power of grief, whether melancholic or worked through, is undeniable. Grief can strip us of those very qualities by which we distinguish ourselves as humans—our ability to speak, to reason, to explain—and as individuals. Those of us who have lived with animals are "undone" by the animals we have lost, and many have witnessed animals who similarly seem to lose part of themselves when they lose their friends—whether "guardians" or "siblings" (biological or acquired). Both LaCapra and Butler understand grief and mourning to have an ethical valence because they foreground our shared vulnerability and interdependence and consequently remind us of our responsibility to others. This responsibility, I believe, is especially significant with regard to others whose vulnerability is greater than ours. Both LaCapra and Butler want to insist, moreover, that the power of grief need not be privatizing or render us passive.[51] Indeed, for LaCapra, the ethical potential of mourning is a function of the activity of "working through" such that "affirmed vulnerability . . . does not exclude agency."[52] Nevertheless, the responses to grief, as to the realization of shared vulnerability (as humans and animals), are varied, bringing some to build a communal response to violence, as Butler argues, and leading others to assert boundaries of difference that allow for preemptive strikes or for what Derrida might express in terms of eating the other before becoming a meal oneself.[53]

"Let's face it. We're undone by each other," Butler writes. "And if we're not, we're missing something."[54] When Klein says that a "dog should die like a dog," he denies the fact that we humans often grieve the dogs and other animals we live with—grieve them not necessarily because they are humanized, but because they do transcend boundaries of kin and kind by becoming integral to our lives as social partners rather than as resources. Woolf and Mann and Tolstoy understood this, even as their modernist works respect species differences in their representations of animal deaths. The postmodernist becomings in Taylor-Wood's video and Cixous's story work to dislodge the representations of death and by extension the ethics of grief from the anthropocentric prejudices of species difference. But they do so by destabilizing and perhaps disabling the representations of those who may be and should be grieved.

7

. . . .

THINKING AND
UNTHINKING
ANIMAL DEATH

Temple Grandin and J. M. Coetzee

Death, Disability, Deflection

Woolf's Flush died of "natural causes." Tolstoy's Strider was killed.
What is the significance of that difference given that both died pain-
lessly and at an old age? One result of the ethical turn in the animal
question has been a turning away from a focus on ontological distinctions between those who know death and those who, as Heidegger
says, merely "perish," and a turning toward questions of killing and of
how and under what conditions an animal can be killed with impunity.
Focusing on the situatedness of ethics, philosophers such as Jacques
Derrida and Emmanuel Levinas have advocated the importance of
moving away from generalizeable, institutional, or "calculable" laws
for moral action to a focus on the suffering of those who have been
victims of violent acts. The distinction bears similarities to the distinction between Kant's understanding of moral theory as dependent
on the autonomy of the moral subject and Hegel's notion of the ethical life as always intersubjective, directed to the life of another, especially to a vulnerable other.[1] To prioritize our subjective (and messy)
interdependence, according to much of current theory and literature, entails a stripping of autonomous selfhood or at least an undoing of those capacities for rational thinking, language, and agency
that are said to determine ethical laws. To follow such laws without

experiencing the emotional confusion that they attempt to resolve is thus to act obediently, even like a dog some would say, but not to act out of the necessary difficulty that an ethical choice would entail. Ethical behavior, in such a view, must be distinguished from the unthinking behavior associated with animals.

Of course, the ethical status of killing has always depended on ontological distinctions, such that murder, as Derrida reminds us, and the commandment "Thou shall not kill" are understood to apply to humans alone. But the fact is that human and nonhuman animals alike have at various times been "made killable," to use Donna Haraway's phrase. Moreover, Haraway suggests, in a world where to eat is to kill and to deplete resources for others and where to live is necessarily to live off another, it may be "a misstep to pretend to live outside killing." "The problem is not figuring out to whom such a command applies so that the 'other' killing can go on as usual and reach unprecedented historical proportions. The problem is to learn to live responsibly within the multiplicitous necessity and labor of killing, so as to be in the open, in quest of the capacity to respond in relentless historical, nonteleological, multispecies contingency. Perhaps the commandment should read, 'Thou shalt not make killable.'"[2]

As opposed to "making killable," Haraway proposes that we think instead about "killing well"—a concept that she builds around Derrida's notion of "eating well."[3] Both ideas begin with the premise that "we all must eat" and that eating, like living, entails feeding off another's life or livelihood. Both Haraway and Derrida, however, attempt to think outside the humanist, "sacrificial structure" whereby only some are "made killable" or, as Derrida explains, whereby the line between a criminal and "non-criminal putting to death" is drawn by the giving of a name (the name of the animal), by the invocation of an a priori moral law, or by a "calculation" of costs versus benefits. Thus, with regard to "killing well," Haraway writes of the need to learn to kill and be killed responsibly, "yearning for the capacity to respond and to recognize response, always with reasons, but always knowing there will never be sufficient reason."[4] Derrida similarly emphasizes that there can be no truly responsible or ethical act that does not pass through the proofs of the "incalculable" or the "undecidable."[5] Otherwise, ethics would not be a response at all, but the application of a rule or mathematical equation; it would be more of a "reaction" than a "response" and hence an opting out of responsibility.[6]

The insufficiency of reason and thought for providing an ethics of killing and eating as well as the importance of acknowledging and experiencing our concomitant vulnerability in this regard are the subject of a profoundly moving essay by Cora Diamond. Borrowing the term *exposure* from Stanley Cavell, Diamond writes of the importance of our sense of exposure to "sheer animal vulnerability, the vulnerability we share with them." That exposure may make us panic, she admits, and part of why we panic is that we cannot put into words either what it is exactly that affects us so or how to respond to it. The very "difficulty of reality," Diamond says, is what makes "reality resistant to our thinking it, or painful in its inexplicability."[7] And yet, she suggests, the experience of such difficulty must be the foundation of any ethics.

Insofar as we humans are often very good at avoiding such exposure, the turn to animals or, as I consider here as well, to the alternately abled is a turn to learn from those who have fewer possibilities for escaping from such exposure and may have developed other means or modes of getting their minds around it. This is one reason why animal studies has come of age in conjunction with a so-called counterlinguistic turn. Although many current projects are intent on proving that certain animals do have language capabilities like those of humans, other sectors of animal studies are concerned with forms of subjectivity that are not language based. They are instead concerned with ways of knowing that appear to work outside those processes of logocentric, rational thinking that have defined what is proper to the human as opposed to the nonhuman animal. These concerns are also shared by a subset of disability studies that focuses on persons with so-called disorders that manifest themselves linguistically, such as Asperger's syndrome and autism. Temple Grandin's work has been exemplary in this respect, perhaps because she is so keenly aware of the way her autism challenges preconceived ideas of what constitutes rational thought. "I think in pictures," she writes in the beginning of her second book, *Thinking in Pictures.* "Words are like a second language to me." Moreover, she emphasizes, "I would be denied the ability to think by scientists who maintain that language is essential for thinking."[8]

Grandin's work is especially compelling for the postlinguistic turn because of the way she turns her linguistic disability into a special ability or gift.[9] She claims that her autism has given her special insight into the minds of nonhuman animals, cattle in particular. In addition to a greater sensitivity to touch that allows her to read cows' and horses' body language with her fingers, she maintains that she is able to see what and how nonhuman animals see. In her third book, *Animals in Translation*, Grandin goes even further to point out the visual impairment of so-called normal humans because of an overactive consciousness that screens out much of what is before them. She cites a study in which test subjects were asked to watch a basketball game and count the number of passes made by one member of the teams. Focused on the task, 50 percent of those watching did not notice a woman in a gorilla suit who walked onto the screen and began to pound her chest. "It's not that normal people don't see the lady dressed in a gorilla suit at all," Grandin writes; "it's that their brains screen her out before she reaches consciousness."[10]

Where Grandin speaks of "screening," Cora Diamond writes of "deflection" in order to describe the ways we avoid ideas that we are unprepared to think either because they aren't logical or because they are too painful. According to Diamond, ethical reasoning may itself be a deflection from the very "duty of moral thinking," a duty that above all means *not* deflecting our exposure to the world, but rather forcing ourselves to experience the confusing and wounding "difficulty of reality."[11] For the early-twentieth-century German poet Rainer Maria Rilke, screening and deflection are included in the "world" that structures and shapes our vision of reality, thereby reducing the intensity of that world's hold on us. For Rilke, these aspects of the world get in the way, diminish what we take in from reality, and, he suggests furthermore, prevent us from seeing what animals see. Articulating a critical perspective that Martin Heidegger will challenge, Rilke claims that humans are disadvantaged by their consciousness and unable to perceive "the open" that is available to animal eyes.

With all its eyes the creature–world beholds
The open. But our eyes, as though reversed
Encircle it on every side, like traps
Set round its unobstructed path to freedom.[12]

Rilke's "Eighth Elegy" articulates already in 1922 what seems to have become an increasingly powerful, contemporary notion—one that is both mournful and hopeful—that (1) human consciousness is an obstacle to a knowledge we may have once possessed—a larger, less circumscribed, and less rational way of knowing—and (2) it may be possible if not to retrieve, then to imagine a fullness of vision in poetry or through the eyes of those who are removed from "normal" sociolinguistic behavior, whether nonhuman animals or persons with certain linguistic and cognitive disabilities. For Elizabeth Costello, the protagonist of J. M. Coetzee's *Lives of Animals*, poetry is best suited to these animals' or persons' task of accessing this knowledge because it is not dependent on reason for its insights and because reason is "not the being of the universe, but on the contrary merely the being of the human brain."[13] Reason, Costello argues, is a tautological structure that represents only a "small spectrum of human thinking" and dismisses animals either as silent or as speaking in unreasonable or unthinking ways that need not be listened to. In her lectures, Costello opposes the truths of reason and philosophy to the insights of poetry and the empathic imagination that poetry depends on. She describes Ted Hughes poem "The Jaguar" as "poetry that does not try to find an idea in the animal or that is not about the animal, but is instead a record of engagement with him."[14] The goal of such poetry, in other words, is to engage the animal not as an object over which the poet and poem establish a certain knowledge or mastery, but rather as a subjective interlocutor whose very being shares in the creative force behind the poem.

Costello thus echoes Rilke's skepticism regarding the language of reason, which she regards less a tool of mastery than of masking weakness. Paraphrasing Jacques Lacan, Derrida writes, "Man is an animal, but a speaking one, and he is less a beast of prey than a beast that is prey to language."[15] In other words, what is proper to man (and presumably to woman) is to be caught, if not trapped, by his own words and the world they enforce. This is a crucial point in Derrida's

· · · · · · · · · · · ·

120

critiques of Heidegger, whose obstinate humanism, Derrida contends, is built upon essentializing terms such as *the animal* in order to draw false and dangerous boundaries between them and us. In his essay *The Animal That Therefore I Am*, Derrida turns Heidegger's hierarchy upside down; where Heidegger sees human language as the mark of our superiority over animals, Derrida asks us to consider whether the animal's apparent "lack" of language is indeed a lack. "It would not be a matter of 'giving speech back' to animals, but perhaps of acceding to a thinking, however fabulous and chimerical it might be, that thinks the absence of the name and of the word otherwise, as something other than a privation."[16]

The hunch that human language may be an obstacle to knowing and that, therefore, those who are somehow outside the symbolic may have access to domains that humans cannot know may also explain why the counterlinguistic turn is contemporaneous with particular attention to death and the act of putting to death. This has been the case not only in reference to right-to-life issues, but also with regard to a philosophical reevaluation of the human as the only animal who knows death "as such." Heidegger attributes this knowledge, if obliquely, to the human faculty of speech. "Mortals are they who can experience death as death. Animals cannot do this. But animals cannot speak either. The essential relation between death and language flashes up before us, but remains still unthought."[17] The precise relation of death to language, as Derrida comments, and what it might mean for any being to have access to death "as such" without actually dying are unclear.

Here again Heidegger reverses Rilke's privileging of the animal's freedom from death. "We, only, can see death," Rilke writes in "The Eighth Elegy." The English translation appears to emphasize the exclusive status of vision—we only *see* it, whereas the German, "*Ihn,* sehen wir allein," emphasizes that "death is all we see"—like the world of objects that obstructs our vision of the "open." Only when we are in fact "near death" does our sight see beyond it: "For, nearing death, one perceives death no longer, / And stares ahead—perhaps with large brute gaze."[18] And then, we must assume, we see no more.

Only death brings us close to the brute or animal gaze (*Tierblick*). But whose death: our own or the death of another? What about the death of an animal that for many of us is the first encounter we have with death and with killing, whether it be the fly we swat, the lobster we see dropped into boiling water, or the pet that we euthanize? Do these deaths count as knowledge of death "as such," or do they somehow change the stakes of that knowledge? What exactly might an animal death do for us—not in terms of what it might supply us as food or clothing, but rather in terms of any "knowledge" gained from seeing an animal die, if not from killing it ourselves? These questions come in part out of what we know to be the relative invisibility of the enormous numbers of animal killings that take place daily in slaughter yards, science labs, and animal shelters—killings that before the middle of the nineteenth century most often took place before our eyes on the streets, if not in the kitchen. The look of the animal that, according to John Berger,[19] we have lost in the past century may also be the look of the animal we kill—whether for slaughter, for sport, or perhaps out of mercy.[20] The importance of this look is nevertheless one that Grandin foregrounds in a section of her own book that deals with her work in slaughter yards. Her description of this killing bears striking similarities to a moment in Coetzee's novel *Disgrace*, especially in its appeal to a realm beyond what can be thought. Coetzee's writing has wrestled with questions of animals and death for at least the past decade, and in this novel the look of the animal we kill provokes, however disturbingly, a transforming moment in the life of the main protagonist, David Lurie, as I discuss in what follows.

Killing Well?

In the concluding discussion of the recent volume of essays entitled *Killing Animals* by the Animal Studies Group, Jonathan Burt states, "It's almost as though the closer and closer you get to animal killing the more everything begins to fall apart, perspective and everything." "And language," adds Steve Baker.[21] Indeed, in Grandin and Coetzee's work we find that killing animals brings us face to face with the inadequacies of our language or at least with the rational and logical thinking it enables. Death, as in the death of Sam Taylor-Wood's hare in *A Little Death*, is the place where the conceptual and ontological distinctions that language makes possible break down—including the distinctions between human and animal. But also apparent in Grandin and Coetzee's writings is that everything also comes together around the right kind of animal killing in a way that is at once elemental and religious—at least for the persons directly involved. For their readers, on the contrary, what falls apart is a framework for judging those killings, especially as we are witnesses to conversion experiences precipitated by what most interpretations would count as a "good death," a euthanasia. But what is a good death, and whom or what does it serve?

Toward the beginning of *Thinking in Pictures*, Temple Grandin tells of a "breakthrough" she had while assisting in the act of slaughter at a kosher plant that she had redesigned. Having replaced a cruel system of hanging live cattle upside down by one leg with a kind of hydraulic "squeeze machine" into which the cattle would enter one by one and be held calmly in place for the rabbi to perform the final deed, she tries out the controls of the hydraulic machinery herself, working the levers as if they were extensions of her own body.

> Though the machine I reached out and held the animal. When I held his head in the yoke, I imagined placing my hands on his forehead and under his chin and gently easing him into position. Body boundaries seemed to disappear, and I had no awareness of pushing the levers. The rear pusher gate and head yoke became an extension of my hands. . . .
>
> During this intense period of concentration I no longer heard noise from the plant machinery. I didn't feel the sweltering Alabama summer heat, and everything seemed quiet and serene. It was almost a religious experience. It was my job to hold the animal gently, and it was the rabbi's job to perform the final deed. I was able to look at each animal, to hold him gently and make him as comfortable as possible during the last moments of his life. I had participated in the ancient slaughter ritual the way it was supposed to be. A new door had been opened. It felt like walking on water.[22]

This passage is remarkable for a number of reasons. First, as Grandin herself emphasizes, is the revalorizing of what is generally understood to be a disability. The "problems" autistics have with body boundaries and knowing, for instance, where the body ends and the chair begins here become an enabling force that allows her to become one with the machine, if not with the animal.[23] Second, of course, is the act of slaughter itself. Here, technology is not an evil force, but rather that which, when lovingly implemented (as Grandin describes), allows for an untraumatic and painless death for the animal and something of a religious epiphany for Grandin—indeed, a Heideggerean "revealing" of Being. "As the life force left the animal, I had deep religious feelings. For the first time in my life logic had been completely overwhelmed with feelings I didn't know I had."[24] It must be remembered, however, that in all this breakdown of boundaries between human, machine, and animal, what remains unaffected is the sacrificial structure that violently reestablishes those boundaries at the moment they appear to be effaced. It is, of course, the animal alone who dies or at least perishes. My point here is not to find fault with Grandin, who has done much to improve the handling of cattle, but to draw attention to the scene's contradictory and competing interests.

A similar problematic is at the heart of the novel *Disgrace*, and although Coetzee, unlike Grandin, is an avowed vegetarian, that novel seems also to suggest that some sort of "grace" can be found through animal sacrifice, if not through the right killing of animals. This "grace," moreover, is the culmination of the protagonist's transformation from one who abjects animals (and women) to one who recognizes himself in animals. We may remember that David Lurie is, at least in the beginning of the novel, a wholly despicable character—a university professor of literature with a bothersome sexual appetite that he feeds with prostitutes and students. He considers animals, like women, soulless creatures who exist to satisfy him: they "do not own themselves," he thinks to himself when looking at a pair of tethered sheep. "They exist to be used, every last ounce of them, their flesh to be eaten, their bones to be crushed and fed to poultry."[25]

Lurie, however, experiences a change with regard both to the animals around him and to his own "animal" nature once he is charged with sexual harassment and forced to retreat to his daughter Lucy's farm. The animals on that farm and in particular those animals who are in their "grace period"—the time they have before being put down or slaughtered for food—begin to have an odd and inexplicable effect on him. It begins with the same two sheep: "suddenly and without reason, their lot has become important to him." "I am disturbed," he says, "I cannot say why" (126–127). This irrational bond is deepened when Lurie begins to help Lucy's friend Bev euthanize sickly and unwanted dogs and cats in a local clinic. As if overwhelmed by what happens in this "theater," as he calls it, he is slowly drawn to devote his life to the death of the animals, ensuring that they die with his full attention and, indeed, with his love—a word that Grandin also uses and that it seems both Grandin and Lurie experience only in the silent act of killing. "He and Bev do not speak. He has learned by now, from her, to concentrate all his attention on the animal they are killing, giving it what he no longer has difficulty in calling by its proper name: love" (219).

Lurie, like Grandin, experiences a certain communion with animals through the retrieval of that lost look at the moment of death. Like Grandin, moreover, Lurie associates modern technology not with mass slaughter and factory farming, but rather with a death that individualizes and offers to each victim the recognition that their lives seem to have denied them. Technology is less a means of instrumentalizing, less a tool of mastery, than a force by which Lurie slowly comes to sense a slow unraveling of mastery and comprehension.

> He had thought he would get used to it. But that is not what happens. The more killings he assists in, the more jittery he gets. One Sunday evening, driving home in Lucy's kombi, he actually has to stop at the roadside to recover himself. Tears flow down his face that he cannot stop; his hands shake.
> He does not understand what is happening. (143)

Whereas for Claude Lévi-Strauss animals are good to think, for Coetzee killing animals is good to unthink, to strip us of the rational and metaphysical assumptions by which we have distinguished ourselves from animals. It is in the animal clinic, in the "theater" where the performance of life is enacted through a putting to death, that Lurie begins to value what Italian philosopher Giorgio Agamben calls "bare life," a zone of indistinction between human and animal.[26] It is "bare life" that Lurie first experiences when four intruders beat him, rape Lucy, and kill her dogs. And it is that life—the one that, as Lucy says "we share with animals" (74)—that Lurie begins to devote himself to as he tends to proper burials for each animal, making sure that their corpses "will not be beaten into a more convenient shape for processing" (143). Calling himself a "dog-man," Lurie takes heed of his own creatureliness and in particular of his smell—the smell he gives off to the dogs in the clinic, the smell, he says, of his thoughts. As "world" begins to fade around him, he becomes in effect captivated by the dogs, as by the unformed music in his head—*captivation* being the word that Agamben borrows from Heidegger to describe the animal's being open to its environment, "ecstatically drawn outside of itself,"[27] even if it cannot know it. It is in this state that Lurie, like Grandin, senses the overwhelming if irrational need to respond not only to the animals' suffering, but even more so to an unfathomable absence of Being that, because of our shared mortality, we will also share with animals in death. "Mortality," writes Derrida, "resides there, as the most radical means of thinking the finitude that we share with animals, the mortality that belongs to the very finitude of life, to the experience of compassion, to the possibility of sharing the possibility of this nonpower, the possibility of this impossibility, the anguish of this vulnerability and the vulnerability of this anguish."[28] "*Du musst dein leben åndern*: you must change your life" (209), Lurie says to himself, citing Rilke's famous line about the power of art, if not the intense power of a headless body.[29]

Like art, animals call us (pace Levinas)[30] to witness our own and the other's time-bound, vulnerable existence. But how does this experience change our lives? It seems surprising, if not contradictory, that for both Grandin and Lurie communion with animal suffering leads not to "the sacrifice of sacrifice"—that is to say, to the condemnation of a noncriminal killing of animals—but rather to the embracing of such sacrifice in its lost ritualistic aspects, its lost look. "There is a need," writes Grandin, "to bring ritual into the conventional slaughter plants and use it as a mean to shape people's behavior. It would help people from becoming numbed, callous, or cruel. The ritual could be something very simple, such as a moment of silence. . . . No words. Just one pure moment of silence. I can picture it perfectly."[31]

The very end of *Disgrace* similarly makes an appeal to the ritual of sacrifice as Lurie decides to end the grace period of the one dog for whom he began to have a real fondness, the dog who became the sole audience for his music, the dog who, he says, "would die for him."

> He opens the cage door. "Come," he says, bends, opens his arms. The dog wags its crippled rear, sniffs his face, licks his cheeks, his lips, his ears. He does nothing to stop it. "Come."
>
> Bearing him in his arms like a lamb, he re-enters the surgery. "I thought you would save him for another week," says Bev Shaw. "Are you giving him up?"
>
> "Yes, I am giving him up." (220)

Thus, in both Grandin and Coetzee, the attention to animals founds a kind of posthumanist religiosity, as if each were called, although by whom and for what is unclear. "For the sake of the dogs? But the dogs are dead; and what do dogs know of honor and dishonor anyway?" Lurie ponders (146). Indeed, the very ritual that acknowledges the animal's Being or soul also undergirds the sacrificial and logocentric structure and puts the human back at the center. "The sacrificial animal," Nietzsche writes, "does not share the spectator's ideas about sacrifice, but one has never let it have its say."[32]

If it did speak, though, could we understand it?

Part IV

· ·

ETHICAL
BÊTISES

8

. . . .

ANIMAL LIBERATION OR
SHAMELESS FREEDOM

Bêtises and the Difficulty of Reality

Insofar as our engagements with animals bring us to think or, rather, to unthink—if we learn the lessons of Temple Grandin and David Lurie—they can have an immensely powerful effect. But the ethical demands produced by these encounters may be equally unfathomable. In response to the "impossibility of reality" and to the intensity of experiences that neither can quite understand, both Grandin and Lurie work within the system to make a difference to individual animals, one by one. For many, however, the difference they make is not enough. Indeed, many would regard their responses as deflections from the system that legitimates animal sacrifice, if not our sovereignty over animals. It is understandable, states Steve Baker, "that the focus has been on the so-called humanity, or lack of humanity, of the killing of the individual animal within slaughterhouse practices, because what is unthinkable is the scale of the whole industry and all its economic, social and cultural ramifications. That's too big a thing to take on." Comparing the pet industry to the meat industry, Jonathan Burt adds, "We have to embed the question of pets into the mass of human–animal relations rather than individualizing it."[1]

Burt points out how "slaughter in a sort of secular, 'high-tech' society is full of . . . religious sentiments,"[2] referring presumably to the sacrificial structure at the base of the industry. Such religious senti-ments are the driving force behind Matthew Scully's attempts to take on the system in his book *Dominion: The Power of Man, the Suffer-ing of Animals.* Within the Judeo-Christian tradition, "dominion" is our "first calling," Scully reminds his readers, even as the term has been misunderstood and misused.[3] In his sympathetic and persuasive accounts of the systematic wrongs done to animals in slaughter, fish-ing, and safaris, Scully understands dominion as predicated upon our human ability to make "moral" judgments—something animals can-not do. We have a moral imperative to take responsibility for animals in the form of stewardship rather than domination. "Someone has to assume dominion, and looking around the earth we seem to be the best candidates, exactly because we humans are infinitely superior in reason and alone capable of knowing justice under a dominion still greater than our own."[4]

Scully's attempt to distinguish dominion from domination in order to promote a platform of animal welfare has been criticized by so-called animal abolitionists, who regard such animal welfare as a Band-Aid masking the fundamental problem of corrupt and unjust human sovereignty in the world.[5] This is especially the case for domestic ani-mals, the abolitionists argue, who have been "made" by humans and thus can only ever be exploited and controlled objects of human use. The system, they argue, can be taken on only by abolishing it. But the danger of such Marxist-inspired approaches to questions of domes-tication is that they deny the potential for any meaningful interac-tion between human and nonhuman animals; they refuse the "web of interspecies dependencies"[6] of which we all are a part. Indeed, what appears to link the welfarists to the abolitionists is their common acceptance of "human exceptionalism," whereby man, as a political (and ethical) animal, stands outside (either above or below) any nec-essary (or dependent) relation to other species—the former by under-standing sovereignty as the essence of our ethical humanity, the latter by regarding sovereignty as the essence of our ignoble animality.

In *The Beast and the Sovereign,* Derrida points to this double and contradictory figuration of man as a "political animal" whose sover-eignty is both a function of and opposed to his status as animal. "Just where the animal realm is so often opposed to the human realm as the realm of the nonpolitical to the realm of the political, and just where it has seemed possible to define man as a political animal or living being, a living being that is, on top of that, a 'political' being, there too the essence of the political, and in particular of the state and sovereignty has often been represented in the formless form of animal monstrosity . . . an artificial monstrosity of the animal."[7] All of which is to say that the difficulty of the concept of "killing well" that I discussed in chapter 7 is one version of the "difficulty of reality" and that both issue from the inescapability of our *bêtise*, the term that Derrida, following Deleuze and Flaubert, uses to refer to that particular animality that only humans experience. "Bêtise" is that combination of knowledge and lack of understanding, of cruelty and impassivity, that is "proper" to man because of his sovereignty, because he believes that he is free to do otherwise than kill and be cruel—and because, in some instances, he cannot do otherwise. Derrida tries to come to grips with this bestial quality that is "proper" to man (animals cannot be "bêtes"), even as he admits that the "compulsion to know *bêtise* . . . is *bête*" itself.[8] He quotes Deleuze directly: "Perhaps this is the origin of the melancholy that weighs down on the finest human figures: the presentiment of a hideousness proper to the human face, a rise of *bêtise*, a deformation in evil, a reflection in madness. For from the point of view of a philosophy of nature, madness rises up at the point at which the individual reflects himself in this free ground, and consequently, then, *bêtise* in *bêtise*, cruelty in cruelty, and cannot stand himself any longer."[9]

As we humans see ourselves and our acts reflected in the more than human world, we see reflections of a bêtise that is as much a result of our unjust sovereignty over other animals as of our (unacknowledged) lack of sovereignty over ourselves. What may be most frightening is the realization that even our attempts at kindness can be *bêtes* (perhaps, as some say, our morality itself stems from our "animal" instincts) and that they can do harm even when we believe we are doing what is right. Indeed, the greatest *bêtise*, according to Derrida, may be believing that we are protected from doing wrong by our philosophical and ethical certainties—by our moral categories; "the category," Derrida reminds us, is "a signature of *bêtise*."[10] It is in constructing exclusive categories of right and wrong or of human and animal that we refuse the "contagion" of our condition as human animals. Just as Derrida, following Flaubert, writes about a "compulsion for intelligence" that is itself *bête* (especially in separating intelligence from what is animal), so in this chapter I write about an ethical compulsion that is driven by a refusal of the deep bonds of affection we share with at least some animals and of the possibility that they, too, may accept those bonds as the price (and sometimes the point) of life. "All too often men are betrayed by the word, freedom," says Kafka's ape.[11] It is imperative that we not confuse ethics with a liberation that cleanses us humans of our sovereignty (and its presumed "animality") only by denying the "humanity" we share with animals.

For His Idea of the World

Derrida writes that "the best literature, for its part ('best' is Deleuze's word), . . . even if it does not treat thematically and systematically the *bêtise* of thought, *bêtise* as a structure of thought, lets itself be haunted by *bêtise*, haunted by the 'problem of *bêtise*.'"[12] It is in this respect that I want to return to Coetzee's *Disgrace*—a novel haunted by this problem, much as the novel's ending can be said to haunt its readers. This baffling ending illustrates the confusing ethical situations that issue from the "difficulty of reality." In the final scene, as I mentioned in chapter 7, the previously unlikeable protagonist David Lurie "gives up" the one dog with whom he had developed a relationship. That dog, much like Lurie himself, is unwanted and beaten by life but nevertheless, as Lurie knows, "would die for him." "Bearing him in his arms like a lamb,"[13] Lurie determines the dog's time has come and offers him up to be euthanized. But why?

In a review of the novel, Ian Hacking writes of this sacrificial gesture, "I cannot comprehend [it], and only barely feel it as possible."[14] Josephine Donovan admits that Coetzee does come close to aestheticizing evil in this scene but adds that she has chosen "to interpret the scene within the evident ethical context [she believes] Coetzee intends" and in which his protagonist can "experience a conversion to a heightened state of moral awareness."[15] In an opposing view, David Attridge warns against reading Lurie's behavior as any kind of conversion to an "ethical response" to animal suffering. "This is not a practical commitment to improving the world, but a profound need to preserve the integrity of the self."[16] Refusing to find any such conversion in Lurie's character, Attridge reads Lurie's life as consistently living for an idea—an idea that has little to do with the dog. This is indeed how Lurie reportedly answers his own question about why he has taken on the job of giving the euthanized dogs an honorable cremation. "But the dogs are dead; and what do the dogs know of honor and dishonor anyway?—For himself, then, for his idea of the world, a world in which men do not use shovels to beat corpses into a more convenient shape for processing" (146). Like Attridge, Louis Tremaine resists reading Lurie's gesture as ethical but does find that it marks an important change in his character. Tremaine suggests in opposition to Attridge that for the first time Lurie is able to see the dog in terms of its "own conditions of existence, without imposing his own idea of it . . . the dog is 'just a dog,' and David is just a human being—body–souls, animals both of them—and he cannot save either of them by rendering them into art."[17] Tremaine thus sees the ending as a beginning for Lurie, who in response to the crippled dog is finally able to come to terms with the "shame of suffering and of death" that no artistic project can relieve. But why, I have to ask, is the dog's death or any death shameful, and is not shame an idea?

I thought of this ending again after reading and hearing a paper titled "Animal Welfare and the Moral Value of Nonhuman Animals" by Gary Francione, Distinguished Professor of Law at Rutgers University. The major premise of his paper is that the animal welfare position— that "it is morally acceptable to use animals as human resources as long as we treat them 'humanely' and do not inflict 'unnecessary suffering' on them"—provides "an insignificant level of protection to nonhuman animals." More specifically, Francione argues that the welfare position supports the view that "the life of nonhumans has lesser moral value than the life of humans" and thus acts as a justification for using nonhumans as resources or "chattel property."[18] This point makes some sense and, indeed, is one reason why some municipalities in the United States are changing the designation of those who live with companion animals from *pet owners* to *pet* or *animal guardians*. Francione does not discuss guardianship in this paper, however, or any form of relationship with animals outside of property. Indeed, Francione's ultimate conclusion forecloses any consideration of such relations. Because, he claims, there can be no justification for using animals in ways that we would not condone using humans (a familiar argument against speciesism) and that we nevertheless continue to turn them into property with interests that are necessarily subservient to our own interests as owners, we should stop producing domestic animals at all. "If we took animals seriously and recognized our obligation not to treat them as things, we would stop producing and facilitating the production of domestic animals altogether. We would care for the ones whom we have here now, but we would stop breeding more for human consumption and we would leave non-domesticated animals alone. We would stop eating, wearing, or using animal products and would regard veganism as a clear and unequivocal moral baseline."[19]

As Francione clarified in the discussion following his paper, his conclusion does not mean we should let domestic animals breed on their own. Rather, he declared, we should sterilize all living domestic animals to ensure they all will die out. Only this action will stop the slavery. Only the extinction of all domestic animals—and he made no distinction between animals for food and animals for companionship—is a solution to our wrongs. This solution, I thought, is the law professor's sacrifice of the animals for his "idea of the world."

After hearing the talk, I went back to Coetzee's novel to think again about how to read the ending. I had understood it as depicting Lurie's one and only gesture of love, the proof that he had truly undergone a transformation during the novel and had come to a realization of his abuse of others.[20] In the beginning, Professor Lurie is presented as a self-important, divorced, and aging man who subjects women (including his students) and animals to his desires. He regards both as existing for his own use and pleasure and denies that either might have a right to a life or love of their own. In the course of the novel, however, during which he is dismissed from the university for sexual harassment and then finds himself and his daughter subjected to acts of violence from others, Lurie unaccountably becomes moved by the suffering of the animals he encounters on his daughter's farm and, perhaps through them, to her suffering as well. As he befriends Bev, the woman in charge of the local animal shelter where dogs are abandoned and ultimately euthanized, he insists on accompanying the animals in their final moments and looking into their eyes at the moment of death. Ensuring a proper incineration after the act becomes his new job. It is a job motivated by the realization that to die alone is, in this society, the worst indignity, evidence of a life unloved and unmourned.

In the case of the crippled dog, however, a different reading also presents itself. The narrator mentions that Lurie refrains from calling this dog "his" or giving him a name—"Driepoot" is what Bev calls him. The reader might see this restraint as evidence of his refusal to enter into relationship of ownership or domination with the dog. But in his "giving him up," it is clear that some form of relationship—whether of guardianship or ownership (though on the part of whom it is not certain because Lurie says "he has been adopted" [215] by the dog) or perhaps of love—has already taken place. And Lurie's way of dealing with love, we know from earlier in the novel, is to manage it either by paying for it or otherwise by assuming full control. "I lack the lyrical. I manage love too well" (121), he says as a way of explaining his affair with a student. Love must be worthy of Wordsworth, or it must simply satisfy ones "natural" needs through good management. But the dog neither acts as an inspiration for high lyricism nor satisfies any simple needs of nature. What the dog can offer is a relationship or love of the kind that Lurie for much of his life has refused (and now feels himself drawn into)—"that force that drives the utmost strangers into each other's arms making them kin, kind beyond all prudence" (194). In other words, the relationship with the dog offers a love that is not easily managed—a love or even a friendship that is messy because it cannot always be separated from dependence and power but that is not to be spurned because of that. My point is that it is possible to read the transformation Lurie undergoes as a replacement of his aesthetic ideal with an ideal of justice or morality, but in both cases he sacrifices those around him for that ideal rather than let himself be drawn further into a relation that compromises it.[21] In this way, his ideal is not unlike Francione's—if all relations between humans and domestic animals are relations of master and slave, we must let all the animal slaves die out so that we humans can feel good about ourselves and our purity.

. . . .

Such an ideal, it seems to me, is wrong for a number of reasons. It is shamelessly anthropocentric. It suggests that animals should be extinguished for the sake of humans' moral purity. Would that moral purity not be better served by letting humans die out? This anthropocentrism, moreover, and the moral ideal it upholds are grounded in a false view of history, nature, and evolution. In such a view, history is a process of human agency or activity over nature. As anthropologist Tim Ingold writes, "The story we tell about human exploitation and domestication of animals, is part of a more encompassing story about how humans have risen above and have sought to bring under control, a world of nature that includes their *own animality*." In other words, Ingold adds, "when we speak of domestication as an intervention in nature, humanity's transcendence over the natural world is already presupposed."[22] To propose the extinction of all domestic animals is thus to envision a redemptive "end of history" whereby humans rediscover their moral path through their ultimate transcendence or separation from the natural world.[23]

Let me say, first, that there is much to applaud in Francione's work: his concern for the mistreatment of all nonhuman animals, his insistence that nonhumans partake of the moral community regardless of their cognitive capacities, and, in a related manner, his critique of utilitarian attempts to draw a line according to which rights may be granted—all have merit. But his is also a view that forecloses the significance of the nonhuman world by seeing domestic animals as no more than slaves to their human masters. By focusing on human–animal relations solely in terms of property or master and slave, this view discounts domestic animals' agency and social complexity as well as their desire—for connection, affection, and bonding across species, something we see in our dogs or horses.[24] There is no doubt that humans have abused and continue to abuse such affection, but to suggest that therefore dogs or horses should not exist is like saying women should not exist because men have abused them. It is to deny the ways that human and nonhuman animals alike (and here to speak only of domestic animals is to create another false dichotomy) have evolved together, producing more complex life forms through what biologist Lynn Margulis calls "symbiogenesis," which Haraway defines as "intricate and multidirectional acts of association of and with other life forms."[25] Francione's scenario puts faith instead in what Haraway describes as the "culturally normal fantasy of human exceptionalism . . . the premise that humanity alone is not a spatial and temporal web of interspecies dependencies."[26] This fantasy, for reasons that I discuss in the next section, is one that feminists have been especially vocal in exposing and combating.

Human Exceptionalism and Feminist Entanglements

The belief in human exceptionalism is founded on strict divisions between human and animal or culture and nature and perpetuates a dualist thinking that pits an active human (and masculine) master against a passive (and feminized) animal slave. In such a view, which can be traced at least as far back as Aristotle, women have been identified with animals and nature in their need to be tamed or controlled by the masculine, rational element. Early feminists such as Simone de Beauvoir viewed this identification as a source of women's oppression and promoted a disidentification with those forces of nature, the body and the animal, that were seen to be opposed to the privileged, rational element. De Beauvoir realigned women with the side of the rational master but left the other dichotomies intact. More recently, however, building on the groundbreaking work of Carol Adams and Josephine Donovan that critiqued the mutual subjugation of women and nature, but moving in a direction that is both deconstructive of the oppositions that align women and nature and materialist in its attention to the matter of "naturecultures" (as articulated especially by Bruno Latour and Donna Haraway), feminists have begun to espouse an ethics that "repels presumptions of human mastery" because in a posthumanist world the equation of the world of humans with culture as agency (as opposed to nature as mere matter) is understood to be illusory and, more important, "reduce[s] the stuff of life to mere 'resources' for human consumption."[27] What has come to be known as the material turn in feminist theory is, on the one hand, an attempt to redress the blindness created by the "abjection" of nature on the part of some feminists—their effort to separate themselves from the defilement that is associated with the feminine—and, on the other

· · · · · · · · · · · ·

hand, feminism's consequent embracing of post-structuralism's insistence that the material real is produced by discourse or language.[28] Such a view can only promote the kind of anthropocentrism that Ingold calls to our attention because it discounts the "more than human world" as anything other than a human product. Haraway's most recent work, *When Species Meet*, culminates a career spent trying to critique and correct such views and to find ways to talk about nature, animals, and the material world in other than dualist terms. Along with Karen Barad's *Meeting the Universe Halfway: Quantum Physics and the Entanglement of Matter and Meaning*,[29] Haraway and Latour have influenced an emerging group of "material feminists" who insist on the inseparable entanglement and interactions of the human and nonhuman worlds. As Stacy Alaimo and Susan Hekman explain in their introduction to the collected volume *Material Feminisms*, "[These two writers] are developing theories in which nature is more than a passive social construction but is, rather, an agentic force that interacts with and changes the other elements in the mix, including the human."[30]

In *Disgrace*, it is Lucy, Lurie's daughter, who espouses the view of the entanglement of the human and animal worlds—for better or for worse. "This is the only life there is. Which we share with animals." This view guides the way she lives her life, hoping to improve the lives of animals and "to share some of our human privilege with the beasts" (74). Lurie, however, deliberately resists such a view at first, and if during the novel he is increasingly affected by the sheep awaiting slaughter or the dogs awaiting euthanasia, we can only attribute it to them—to the force of the nonhuman world and the impact it can have on humans. It is through this unwilled and unreasoned force that Lurie begins to experience, if not to acknowledge, his kinship with the animals, a kinship that consists first and foremost in having a body that is part of the world of matter or nature. But this kinship he understands as one of humiliation and disgrace, the shame of growing old, the shame of being the product of a fertile body, the shame of having to face death.[31] Such abjection is what Lurie sees and identifies with in the old, crippled dog whom he euthanizes in what Alice Kuzniar interprets as an act of communion produced through "empathetic shame."[32] Kuzniar praises such empathy as a way of also accepting or acknowledging abjection in oneself rather than disavowing it by projecting it onto an animal. In Lurie's "giving up" the dog, we see the extent to which he is moved to relieve the dog (and perhaps himself as well) of his shameful existence once and for all.

Coetzee's foregrounding of shared, empathic embodiment is one reason that his fictions figure prominently in recent work by feminists from the "care tradition." In their introduction to *The Feminist Care Tradition in Animal Ethics*, Josephine Donovan and Carol Adams cite Coetzee as promoting "an awakening of moral awareness, which requires a kind of visceral empathy for the suffering of others."[33] Such empathy is understood to be a necessary first step in tending to animals, which must be joined by a more analytic, political analysis to understand the causes of suffering. Donovan later relates this kind of empathy to the notion of "attentive love" developed first by Simone Weil and later by Iris Murdoch as a moral reorientation away from the self and to the particular experience of an other. *Attentive love* seems a particularly apt term to describe the euthanizing of dogs in *Disgrace*. Lurie "has learned by now . . . to concentrate all his attention on the animal they are killing, giving it what he no longer has difficulty in calling by its proper name: love" (219). *Attention* and *empathy* are key words in the feminist care tradition, where the emphasis is on the need for an ethic to respond to situated, particular experiences of suffering that are often overlooked by rights-based or ruled-based philosophies. And yet as feminists within the care tradition have themselves advised, empathy can be problematic insofar as it erases boundaries of difference between self and other, assuming that my suffering or, worse, my shame is yours.[34] "Attentive love," as Simone Weil originally described it, is not only the recognition of suffering, but also the recognition of suffering in someone exactly like us.[35] This is how the final scene of *Disgrace* has been read—Lurie identifies with the male dog's suffering and consequently with his shame. Kuzniar writes, for example, that "Coetzee suggests that the embodiment of shame in another can serve as a point of identification and empathy, perhaps even for the expression of compassionate love."[36]

The concept of shame is important to consider not only because it is a central theme in Coetzee's novel (as it is for Derrida, who is mentioned alongside Coetzee in Donovan and Adam's introduction to *The Feminist Care Tradition* as two of the "most influential think-ers of our time"), but also because it is the singular emotion that, at least since Darwin, has been theorized to distinguish humans from animals.[37] Shame depends on both self-consciousness and the sup-posed ability to transcend one's body or one's nature. If freedom is understood, from Aristotle to Sartre, to be the distinctly human pos-sibility of being cause of oneself or not being enslaved to one's body, shame results from the awareness (especially in the face of another) of not living up to this idea of freedom. In Coetzee's writings, as in Derrida's *The Animal That Therefore I Am*, however, shame seems to expose our kinship with animals even at the moment we most wish to deny it. Shame is the fact of our nudity, our bodily being that we can hide but not overcome. Shame, as Emmanuel Levinas writes, depends on "the very Being of our being . . . its incapacity to break with itself."[38] Freedom, then, is an anthropocentric illusion of shamelessness that is blind to the unfreedoms that also determine human lives.

But perhaps the problem is that of regarding freedom and shame as necessarily and absolutely opposed. Freedom, Haraway writes, "can-not be defined as the opposite of necessity if the mindful body in all its thickness is not to be disavowed, with all the vile consequences of such disavowal for those assigned to bodily entrammelment such as women, the colonized, and the whole list of 'others' who cannot live inside the illusion that freedom comes only when work and necessity are shuffled off onto someone else."[39] Indeed, Lurie and his daugh-ter have very different ideas of freedom and consequently of shame. He tells his daughter the story of a pet golden retriever who became unmanageable whenever a bitch was around and was punished so often that eventually "it no longer needed to be beaten. It was ready to punish itself." But Lucy takes issue with the moral of the story. "So males must be allowed to follow their instincts unchecked? Is that the moral?—No, that is not the moral, Lurie responds. What was ignoble . . . was that the dog had begun to hate its own nature. At that point it would have been better to shoot it" (90). Lurie's ethic is that of a Nietzschean self-affirmation: death is better than becoming a shameful exemplar of a domesticated or slave morality. This is how he regards his own situation as well. Having fallen "from grace" into that degraded state that he previously assigned to others, he interiorizes the contempt that he had previously directed outward. Lucy, in contrast, identifies not with the dog who must be restrained, but with that dog who would be victim and thus sees the situation differently. Both before and after her rape, which turns the tables of racism to reveal her and her father's powerlessness before an increasingly powerful class of black men, she refuses to let "subjugation" define her life. For her, there is no enduring shame in having limitations on one's freedom (or having it violently taken away) because she considers neither freedom nor shame to be an absolute. She understands that to live (or to produce life) means giving in to relations that restrict and even at times humiliate. But that, she says, "may be a good point to start from again" (205).[40] For Lucy, it would seem, shame can be overcome and can even be productive. Indeed, it allows her to see what is vulnerable in others (even her rapists) by producing empathy without contempt. If she refuses her father's efforts to save or rescue her by helping her move away, it is because she refuses to accept her predicament, unjust as it is, as a state of shame. The crippled dog, however, cannot refuse.

Lurie's empathy for Driepoot—as for his daughter—is evidence of both his profound transformation and his shortsightedness. From an anthropocentric faith in human exceptionalism, Lurie comes to see shame as an ontological state shared with the others around him. But the line here between empathic suffering and anthropomorphism (or narcissism) is thin, and it is dangerous to believe that love for animals consists only in putting them out of their misery. Philosopher and animal trainer Vicki Hearne has described the "sin of pride" that consists in imagining "that one has unmediated awareness of cruelty" toward or even of the suffering of animals. Hearne is critical of the way that, following Bentham, suffering has become the exclusive focus of the attention of so-called animal lovers or the animal rights movement, as if we all know what suffering consists of and, hence, how to relieve it. In an elegant and polemical reading of the biblical story of Job, who was an upright or, in other terms, "humane man," Hearne explains that Job learns that his "uprightnesses" are "nothing but pedantries beside the . . . sort of thing learned in the contemplation of animals." And this is because "the love of animals is not professed in a catechism of their suffering," she declares, "but in uncanny catechisms of their joys,"[41] joys that can be learned only through attention to and acknowledgment of each animal's particular temperament. In the case of Driepoot, Lurie is moved by his idea of disgrace more than by attention to the dog himself, whose signs of joy——the way, for instance, he "smacks his lips" in time with Lurie's music (215)—or whose signs of building his own world, Hearne would say, Lurie ultimately betrays. He refuses what Haraway calls "the unsettling obligation of curiosity" (a critique she also brings against Derrida and his cat)[42] and turns away from his world to wonder whether he can aestheticize such a creature and cast him in his opera.

To be sure, tending to the joys of another may be equally as demanding as tending to their pain. In either case, it would seem that the responsibilities of such an "adopted" relation are too much for Lurie to bear—more than he can manage and more than he has allowed from any human relation. Animals and in particular domestic animals affect us when offered the possibility of doing so, when not removed from sight in factories or laboratory cages. They move us, they call upon us, and thus they interfere with the will to be wholly free, especially when such freedom is understood as the anthropocentric and masculinist idea of the ability to separate from the body or from physical and emotional dependency. Animals interfere with our "idea of the world" if that idea refuses to see that we all must share the responsibilities of responding to others' vulnerabilities and affections. Perhaps this is why Francione can see freedom for animals only in death.

Hearne, by contrast, would look at Driepoot's musical appreciation and at what she calls the "pieties" and "the unlikely and unsuspected happinesses" of animals and people alike and see them as a "rebuke to moral excesses."[43] Indeed, Lurie is in agreement with Hearne on one thing, that domestic animals are unconcerned with the "uprightness" of human morality, unconcerned with the purity of abstract ideas of freedom or kindness, though they are concerned with the consequences of specific practices.[44] "Freedom," Hearne writes, quoting Emmanuel Levinas, "can never be justified, only rendered just."[45] And like kindness, freedom in our actions toward an animal is rendered just only through knowing that animal over time, in a sustained relation, whether that relationship be one of care, companionship, or work.[46] The ambiguity of Coetzee's ending stems from the fact that

Lurie's acts of euthanasia, in at least one way, are "rendered just." In refusing to allow the animals to die alone and in the individual attention he bestows upon each animal so that he or she may die loved, he makes each life a "grievable life."[47] A "grievable life," according to Judith Butler, is a life that can be properly mourned, a life that, in her terms, is recognized as a human life.[48] Lurie demands at least this final possibility for animal lives, making sure that he will grieve even if no one else will. He does not wish for the animals' disappearance, but to mourn their (and his) shame. In this, he moves in a very different direction from the moral uprightness exhibited by Francione, who in seeing only animal slaves sees no loss in their death. That, in my view, is shameful.

"AND TOTO TOO"

Animal Studies, Posthumanism, and Oz

Readers may remember a climactic moment in the film version of *The Wizard of Oz* when Toto, the dog, pulls the curtain (literally) on the Wizard, revealing not a posthuman, disembodied technogod, but a bumbling and balding man. I'd like to think of this moment as an allegory of animal studies' relation to posthumanism and of posthumanism's place in animal studies. Toto, of course, is the driving force behind Frank Baum's narrative because it is Dorothy's love for the dog that leads her to run away and escape the dreary, moral landscape of Kansas and its arbiter, Miss Gulch. "It was Toto who made Dorothy laugh, and saved her from growing as grey as her surroundings," wrote Baum in the original version of the story,[1] and in the film version we can assume that it was such laughter that made Toto a "menace to the community" who, in Miss Gulch's eyes, had to be eliminated. Only those animals who serve humans in a quantifiably productive manner are allowed in Kansas, and both humans and animals are slaves to Gulch and the land much as the Munchkins were slaves to the wicked witch of the East before her death.

With Toto, then, Dorothy escapes to the Land of Oz, a land where technology, in the form of the Wizard, is believed to be the cure for all ills or to make up for all lacks—a land that is peopled largely by hybrids or cyborgs, where, as Dorothy's three friends illustrate, the line between human (Dorothy), animal (the lion), mineral (the scarecrow made of straw), and machine (the tin man) is unclear and not always significant. Here, moreover, each of the friends will find "moral standing" before the Wizard. A "bad wizard" but a "good man," he will grant each of their wishes: for the scarecrow a brain, for the tin man a heart, and for the lion courage. Or, more precisely, he gives to each the outward symbols of humanity the audience already recognizes that they possess, thereby revealing our dependence on exterior signs for knowing who and what it is to be human. This is why Cary Wolfe calls the human a fundamentally "prosthetic creature" who "has co-evolved with various forms of technicity and materiality, forms that are radically 'not-human' and yet have nevertheless made the human what it is."[2]

The significance of Toto's revelatory move lies in delimiting the posthumanism of Oz as one that opposes the dream of the posthuman as a disembodied, transcendent being who rules over the rest of creation and who, alternatively, can absolve itself of rule by eliminating its dependencies (much like Gary Francione's vision, discussed in chapter 8). Such a dream, as Wolfe also emphasizes, is itself derived from the very prejudices of a humanism and, especially, human exceptionalism that we need to redress by insisting on the intimate entanglement of the human in the material and animal world. That deanimalized dream and its critique have formed the core of this book, in literary works from Kafka's "Report," where Red Peter had to whip the animal out of himself in order to leave his cage and join the ranks of humanity, to Mann's *Man and Dog* and Coetzee's *Disgrace*, whose protagonists strive to manage their own appetites, if not those of their pets, in order to separate themselves from and prove their mastery over the world of nature. And that dream is similarly evident in works of philosophy from Nietzsche's ruminations on animals to Derrida's attempts to follow the "animal he is," like a dog chasing his own tail. To represent nature and the animal world, humanism tells us that we must separate ourselves from it, enclose ourselves in our office—as Bill Viola tries in his video *I Do Not Know What It Is I Am Like*, discussed in chapter 2—in order to know what is out there and to distinguish it from what we think or feel or want to be out there. Only in this way can we achieve what Heidegger also criticizes as the world as picture or spectacle, objectified before us and subject to our measuring tools. From such a perspective, the chimpanzees we see in Frank Noelker's photographs and who appear to call upon us to respond to their plight must be both scientifically and morally suspect, a trick of anthropomorphic empathy. As Kant declares, our modern morality depends on our becoming insensitive to all that may muffle or distort the voice of morality within us. Viola and Noelker thus represent two opposed epistemological and moral stances to nonhuman animals as recently outlined by Émilie Hache and Bruno Latour. Viola takes Kant's "moralism" to task to see what happens if we turn animals into a picture in which neither their gaze nor their calls can reach us. Noelker, in contrast, appears to open himself to what Hache and Latour call the "morality" of Gaia, whereby "the earth enters into a moral relationship with us as we begin to ask ourselves how to treat it well."[3] But moralism is not always an easy stance for humans to maintain and demands its own struggle, whose traces are as visible in Viola as in Kant. Kant's conception of morality creates a problem for moderns, Hache and Latour write; "nature frightens us, it calls out to us with such force that we feel impotent, minute, silent before it. We must learn to become insensitive to its call."[4] We must become insensitive but great and powerful wizards.

Whether we are learning to become insensitive to the more-than-human world or learning how to acknowledge it, the contest between moralism and morality is present in these pages in characters' and authors' various efforts to shut out or screen the voices calling them or, alternately, to acknowledge and learn how to respond to their call. Screening, as we saw with Temple Grandin, is a central force behind modernism and humanism's construction of normative subjectivity. Modern or Kantian morality would explain that the lack of screening is what drives Mann's Tobias Mindernickel or Poe and Maupassant's narrators to madness, if not into impassioned violence. Irrational violence, in this view, is derived from our animal ancestors. We become moral (and modern) by distancing ourselves from "the animal" and thus reducing the possibilities for becoming violent ourselves. The fallacy of this view, exposed as much by Virginia Woolf as by recent scholarship, proves that we may never have been fully modern in this way.[5] Although anthropologists debate whether there is not a specifically human form of violence (such as genocide), and animal lovers protest that dogs exhibit the best of humanity (such as honesty, faithfulness, and the ability to love), we must realize that the word on nature versus culture will never be final. As Priscilla Patton writes, "Violence, like love, results from genetics interacting continuously with environment and learned behaviors: another nature-*and*-nurture issue. Violence and abuse of others are not just impulsive acts, but also highly socialized behaviors"[6] (think of the turnaround made by the wicked witch's flying monkeys after she melts).

Exposing the illusory autonomy of the human and embracing the deep, confusing, and scary entanglement of human, animal, and machine in the world of naturecultures has been the project of a certain postmodernism, as we have seen in the work of Hélène Cixous and Sam Taylor-Wood. In its embrace of a sublime deconstruction, however, that project carries its own risk of drawing us into a state of such overwhelming intensity and conceptual confusion that we are unable to retrieve any ethical stance—whether moralist or of moralism. It displaces the categorical imperative by abolishing boundaries between all the categories of identity—whether of species, of life and death, or of nature and culture. In a similar manner, insofar as posthumanism emphasizes the prosthetic nature of the human, it may unwittingly protect us from acknowledging a distinctly human agency in the invention and use of technologies that destroy nonhuman animals with whom we have coevolved.

The question, then, is how to listen to those voices, how to acknowledge the pleasures and uncertainties of our intimately shared worlds, without being so overwhelmed that we lose the possibility of naming the injustices that are waged in the name of the human. In this regard, we should understand posthumanism not as the death of humanism, but as a necessary rethinking of humanist frameworks, including rethinking what thought is, what agency and autonomy are, in order to further humanism's noble aims. Posthumanism, like Oz, is both post- and prehumanism (and in some instances pre- and postmodern) in that it returns us to the moment of struggle when we can hear those voices surrounding us (the scarecrow, the tin man, the lion, but also the good and bad witches) and can decide to listen to them attentively because they demand and in some instances deserve a response. Indeed, to say that "we" must respond implies some certainty about who that "we" is and thus calls upon the humanist, even if she wishes to respond in a posthumanist, ethical fashion. Such an ethics, then, is one that acknowledges the importance of hearing those voices while understanding that any response will also be a reaction, a function of inherited, unconscious, as well as learned and intended behavior. It is hubris, though, if not bêtise, to believe that our thinking can fully escape humanism or that our thinking does not in the end come back to us as humans (however unspecified the term). We should recall what Elizabeth de Fontenay says on this subject, which I quoted earlier in this book: "We cannot entirely purge ourselves of anthropocentrism" (and here I see anthropocentrism and humanism as intimately linked) "except by taking ourselves for the God of Leibniz who is capable of seeing from all possible perspectives. This egoist, or even speciesist point of view (if one accepts the term) . . . is the effect of our finitude before being the mark of our power."[7]

Dorothy, it would appear, understands and respects this finitude, which is perhaps why her only desire (after seeing that the scarecrow, tin man, and lion have received what they asked for) is only to return home to Kansas. Whereas in Baum's version of the story the masculine trio accept offers to rule over sections of Oz—the Emerald City, the Winkies, and the forest, respectively—Dorothy refuses sovereignty in Oz and returns with Toto to Aunt Em's farm. What, if anything, she will change on the farm or in Kansas we will never know. But in waking up to the certainty of connection and closeness between this world and the world of Oz, haunted and perhaps also delighted by the way those three "human" faces from Oz are present at her bedside, she offers an image of hope. "It is not useless to be reminded," Fontenay also writes, "that a 'being with animal' does not happen on its own and that allowing the animal to haunt our world, to trouble us by its alterity, is perhaps the only way to be truly with the animal, without either instrumentalizing or falsely lending that animal a human face."[8] There is work to be done on the farm; humans and animals must find or be given food and drink and shelter from the next storm, and, at least for the moment, they all are in it together. Having returned from Oz together, Dorothy and Toto may have lost the security of the home they once had, but they are in a better position to make their new home more livable for all.

NOTES

Introduction

1. Jacques Derrida, *The Animal That Therefore I Am*, trans. David Wills, ed. Marie-Louise Mallet (New York: Fordham University Press, 2008), 29.

2. See the discussion of Heidegger in Matthew Callarco, *Zoographies* (New York: Columbia University Press, 2008), 50.

3. Gustave Flaubert, *Oeuvres*, ed. Jean Hytier, 2 vols. (Paris: Gallimard, 1957–1960), 2:239.

4. Jacques Derrida, *The Beast and the Sovereign*, vol. 1, trans. Geoffrey Bennington (Chicago: University of Chicago Press, 2009), 154.

5. Ibid., 157.

6. Claude Lévi-Strauss, *Totemism* (Boston: Beacon Press, 1963), 89.

7. Donna Haraway, *When Species Meet* (Minneapolis: University of Minnesota Press, 2008).

8. Donna Haraway, "A Manifesto for Cyborgs: Science, Technology, and Socialist Feminism in the 1980's," in Elizabeth Weed, ed., *Coming to Terms: Feminism, Theory, Politics* (New York: Routledge, 1989), 174.

9. Giorgio Agamben, *The Open: Man and Animal*, trans. Kevin Attell (Stanford, Calif.: Stanford University Press, 2004), 92.

10. See, for example, Carol Adams, *Neither Man nor Beast: Feminism and the Defense of Animals* (New York: Continuum, 1994); and Carol Adams and Josephine Donovan, eds., *Animals and Women: Feminist Theoretical Explorations* (Durham, N.C.: Duke University Press, 1995).

11. Barbara Herrnstein Smith, "Animal Relations, Difficult Relations," *differences* 15, no. 1 (2004), 15.

12. I take the categories "humanist posthumanism" and "posthumanist posthumanism" from Cary Wolfe, *What Is Posthumanism?* (Minneapolis: University of Minnesota Press, 2010), 124, 166–167. The distinctions Wolfe makes between the artists Eduardo Kac and Sue Coe are similar to those that I make between Viola and Noelker, especially insofar as Noelker, like Coe, depends on a subject who sees and who knows through sight. Viola reminds us that, as Wolfe writes with regard to Kac, "what must be witnessed is not just what we can see but also what we cannot see—indeed *that* we cannot see" (167, emphasis in original). Noelker shows us what is wrong with what and how we do see.

13. Richard Klein, "The Power of Pets," *The New Republic*, July 10, 1995, 23.

14. Judith Butler, *Precarious Life: The Powers of Mourning and Violence* (London: Verso, 2004), 20.

15. Wolfe, *What Is Posthumanism?* 99.

16. Cora Diamond, "The Difficulty of Reality and the Difficulty of Philosophy," in Stanley Cavell, Cora Diamond, John McDowell, Ian Hacking, and Carey Wolfe, *Philosophy and & Animal Life* (New York: Columbia University Press, 2008), 45–46, 74.

17. J. M. Coetzee, *Disgrace* (New York: Penguin, 1999),74.

18. Timothy Morton, "Guest Column: Queer Ecology," *PMLA* 125, no. 2 (March 2010), 275, 277. The volume of essays entitled *Queer Ecologies*, edited by Catriona Mortimer-Sandilands and Bruce Erickson (Bloomington: Indiana University Press, 2010), appeared as I was finishing this book.

19. Morton, "Guest Column."

1. A Report on the Animal Turn

1. Paola Cavalieri and Peter Singer, "A Declaration on Great Apes," in Paola Cavalieri and Peter Singer, eds., *The Great Ape Project* (New York: St. Martin's Press, 1993), 4.

2. In her discussion of the concept of women's rights, Wendy Brown comments that rights are founded on notions of individuality that "are predicated upon a humanism that routinely conceals its gendered, racial and sexual norms." Wendy Brown, "Suffering Rights as Paradoxes," *Constellations* 7, no. 2 (2000), 238.

3. Gayatri Chakravorty, "Can the Subaltern Speak?" in Cary Nelson and Lawrence Grossberg, eds., *Marxism and the Interpretation of Culture*, 271–313 (Urbana: University of Illinois Press, 1988).

4. Franz Kafka, "A Report to an Academy," in *Collected Stories*, ed. Gabriel Josipovici, 195–205 (New York: Knopf, 1993); subsequent citations are given parenthetically in the text.

5. On the problems of speech in relation to trauma, see Michael Bernard-Donals and Richard Glejzer, *Between Witness and Testimony: The Holocaust and the Limits of Representation* (Albany: State University of New York Press, 2000); and see Dominick LaCapra, *History and Its Limits* (Ithaca, N.Y.: Cornell University Press, 2009), 59–89.

6. Costello's identification with Red Peter is not, she says, to be taken "ironically." Rather, it comes from a woundedness the two share as human (or woman) and as animal, a woundedness that makes it impossible for them to deliver the papers they were invited to give. J. M. Coetzee, *The Lives of Animals* (Princeton, N.J.: Princeton University Press, 2003), 18.

7. See my discussion of this point in Lacan's work in Kari Weil, *Androgyny and the Denial of Difference* (Charlottesville: University of Virginia Press, 1992), 5–9.

8. Quoted in Cary Wolfe, "In the Shadow of Wittgenstein's Lion: Language, Ethics, and the Question of the Animal," in Cary Wolfe, ed., *Zoontologies: The Question of the Animal* (Minnesota: University of Minnesota Press, 2003), 1.

9. René Descartes, "Animals Are Machines," in Tom Regan and Peter Singer, eds., *Animal Rights and Human Obligations* (Englewood Cliffs, N.J.: Prentice Hall, 1976), 15.

10. On language acquisition in apes, see R. A. Gardner, B. T. Gardner, and T. E. Van Cantfort, *Teaching Sign Language to Chimpanzees* (Albany: State University of New York Press, 1989); and Sue Savage-Rumbaugh, *Kanzi: The Ape at the Brink of the Human Mind* (New York: Wiley, 1996).

11. Jon Hamilton, "A Voluble Visit with Two Talking Apes," *NPR, Weekend Edition*, July 8, 2006, available at http://www.npr.org/templates/story/story .php?storyId=5503685.

12. *Reaction* and *response* are the terms that Lacan uses to oppose animals' and humans' language capabilities, an opposition that Derrida begins to deconstruct in *The Animal That Therefore I Am*, trans. David Wills, ed. Marie-Louise Mallet (New York: Fordham University Press, 2008), especially in "And Say the Animal Responded," 119–140.

13. Hamilton, "Voluble Visit."

14. Quoted in Margaret Talbot, "Birdbrain, the Woman Behind the Chattiest Parrots," *The New Yorker*, May 12, 2008, available at http://www.newyorker .com/reporting/2008/05/12/080512fa_fact_talbot.

15. Verlyn Klinkenborg, "Alex the Parrot," *New York Times*, September

12, 2007, available at http://www.nytimes.com/2007/09/12/opinion/12wed4. html?scp=1&sq=klinkenborg%20alex&st=cse.

16. Wolfe, "In the Shadow of Wittgenstein's Lion," 1.

17. Vicki Hearne, *Adam's Task: Calling Animals by Name* (Pleasantville, N.Y.: Common Reader Editions, 2000), 42.

18. Paul Patton, "Language, Power, and the Training of Horses," in Wolfe, ed., *Zoontologies*, 91.

19. Ibid., 97.

20. See Jakob von Uexküll, *A Foray Into the Worlds of Animals and Humans*, trans. Joseph D. O'Neil (Minneapolis: University of Minnesota Press, 2010).

21. Quoted in Hearne, *Adam's Task*, 115.

22. See Frederick Jameson, *The Prison-House of Language* (Princeton, N.J.: Princeton University Press, 1975).

23. John Berger, "Why Look at Animals," in *About Looking* (New York: Pantheon, 1980), 9.

24. For some, consciousness should be added to this list, especially if consciousness is understood to be coterminous with or dependent on conceptual or linguistic capacities—a belief that much research on animals (and on infants) would disprove.

25. Steve Baker, *The Postmodern Animal* (London: Reaction Books, 2000), 20.

26. Michel Foucault, "What Is Enlightenment?" in *The Foucault Reader*, ed. Paul Rabinow (New York: Pantheon, 1984), 34.

27. Ibid., 32.

28. Giorgio Agamben, *The Open: Man and Animal*, trans. Kevin Attell (Stanford, Calif.: Stanford University Press, 2004), 93.

29. F. R. Ankersmit, *Sublime Historical Experience* (Stanford, Calif.: Stanford University Press, 2005), 333, emphasis in original.

30. Martin Jay, *Songs of Experience* (Berkeley and Los Angeles: University of California Press, 2005), 257.

31. Gilles Deleuze and Félix Guattari, *A Thousand Plateaus: Capitalism and Schizophrenia*, trans. Brian Massumi (Minneapolis: University of Minnesota Press, 1988), 238.

32. Ibid., 240.

33. Gilles Deleuze and Félix Guattari, *Kafka, Toward a Minor Literature*, trans. Dana Polan (Minneapolis: University of Minnesota Press, 1987), 22.

34. For an excellent discussion of a counterlinguistic or "postlinguistic" turn in literary studies and its relation to sublime/traumatic experience, see James Berger, "Falling Towers and Postmodern Wild Children: Oliver Sacks, Don Delillo, and Turns Against Language," *PMLA* 120, no. 2 (2005): 341–361.

35. Donna Haraway, *When Species Meet* (Minneapolis: University of Minnesota Press, 2008), 30.

36. LaCapra, *History and Its Limits*, 170.

37. This is especially the case in the notion of "*écriture*" put forth by French feminists. See my discussion in Kari Weil, "French Feminism's 'Écriture Féminine,'" in Ellen Rooney, ed., *The Cambridge Companion to Feminist Literary Theory*, 153–171 (Cambridge, U.K.: Cambridge University Press, 2006).

38. Cathy Caruth, *Unclaimed Experience: Trauma, Narrative, and History* (Baltimore: Johns Hopkins University Press, 1996), 108.

39. Kelly Oliver, *Witnessing: Beyond Recognition* (Minneapolis: University of Minnesota Press, 2001), 17.

40. Katherine Hayles, *How We Became Posthuman: Virtual Bodies in Cybernetics, Literature, and Informatics* (Chicago: University of Chicago Press, 1999).

41. Donna Haraway, "A Manifesto for Cyborgs: Science, Technology, and Socialist Feminism in the 1980's," in Elizabeth Weed, ed., *Coming to Terms: Feminism, Theory, Politics* (New York: Routledge, 1989).

42. Barbara Herrnstein-Smith, "Animal Relatives, Difficult Relations," *differences* 15, no. 1 (2004), 15–16.

43. Donna Haraway, *The Companion Species Manifesto* (Chicago: Prickly Paradigm Press, 2003), 5.

44. Like Kelly Oliver's in *Witnessing*, Haraway's ethics plays with the notion of response that is integral to ethical responsibility. Because animals have been denied the capacity to respond (rather than merely react), however, Haraway goes further to invoke Derrida's questioning of whether we really know what it means to respond. See Haraway, *The Companion Species Manifesto*, 71, and Derrida, "And Say the Animal Responded," in *The Animal*.

45. Lorraine Daston and Greg Mitman, "Introduction: The How and Why of Thinking with Animals," in Lorraine Daston and Greg Mitman, eds., *Thinking with Animals: New Perspectives on Anthropomorphism* (New York: Columbia University Press, 2005), 11. I use gendered pronouns to acknowledge that animals also have sexes and sexualities, if not genders.

46. Paul S. White, "The Experimental Animal in Victorian Britain," in Daston and Mitman, eds., *Thinking with Animals*, 79. Lorraine Daston's research would appear to counter Samuel Moyn's argument that empathy is grounded on humanism and necessarily takes humanity as its object. See Samuel Moyn, "Empathy in History, Empathizing with Humanity," *History and Theory* 45, no. 3 (2006): 397–415.

47. Coetzee, *The Lives of Animals*, 34.

· · · · · · · · · · · ·

48. Jill Bennett, *Empathic Vision* (Stanford, Calif.: Stanford University Press, 2005), 10, emphasis in original.

49. Thanks to Ellen Rooney for helping me think through some of these issues.

50. Derrida, *The Animal*, 31.

51. Ibid., 11.

52. Ibid., 29.

53. Jacques Derrida and Elizabeth Roudinesco, *For What Tomorrow . . . a Dialogue*, trans. Jeff Fort (Stanford, Calif.: Stanford University Press 2004), 64.

54. Cary Wolfe, *Animal Rites* (Chicago: University of Chicago Press, 2003), 190, 193.

55. Ibid., 203.

56. Derrida and Roudinesco, *For What Tomorrow*, 73.

57. Ibid., 76.

58. Ibid.

59. For an alternative discussion regarding the value of how animal studies may productively inform women's studies in the classroom, see Lori Gruen and Kari Weil, "Teaching Difference: Sex, Gender, Species," in Margo de Mello, ed., *Teaching the Animal: Human–Animal Studies Across the Disciplines*, 127–145 (New York: Lantern Books, 2010).

60. Cary Wolfe, "Introduction," in Wolfe, ed., *Zoontologies*, xi.

61. What we search for, as Herrnstein-Smith writes, is an "ethical taxonomy" that would help sort out the claims of kinship along with other categories of sameness and difference for establishing our responsibilities to others. See Herrnstein-Smith, "Animal Relatives," 2.

2. Seeing Animals

1. Quoted in James Meek, "ANDi, First GM Primate: Will Humans Be Next?" *The Guardian*, January 12, 2001, available at http://www.guardian.co.uk/science/2001/jan/12/genetics.internationalnews.

2. Friedrich Nietzsche, *The Use and Abuse of History*, trans. Adrian Collins (New York: Macmillan, 1957), 5. I discuss Nietzsche's work at greater length in chapter 4.

3. Jacques Derrida, *The Animal That Therefore I Am*, trans. David Wills, ed. Marie-Louise Mallet (New York: Fordham University Press, 2008), 32.

4. Ibid., 29.

5. Thomas Nagel, "What Is It Like to Be a Bat?" *Philosophical Review* 83, no. 4 (October 1974): 435–450; I used the version given at http://members.aol.com/NeoNoetics/Nagel_Bat.html, p. 4.

6. Ibid., 3.

7. Aristotle, "Animals and Slavery," in Tom Regan and Peter Singer, eds., *Animal Rights and Human Obligations* (Upper Saddle River, N.J.: Prentice Hall, 1989), 4.

8. René Descartes, "Animals Are Machines," in Regan and Singer, eds., *Animal Rights*, 14.

9. Nagel, "What Is It Like to Be a Bat?" 2, 3.

10. In this respect, we might say that we humans are "not all" in comparison with animals, much as Lacan wrote that women were "not all" in relation to men because they lack the penis. Jacques Lacan, "God and the *Jouissance* of the̶ Woman," in *Feminine Sexuality: Jacques Lacan and the École freudienne*, trans. Jacqueline Rose, ed. Juliet Mitchell and Jacqueline Rose (New York; Norton, 1982), 144.

11. Martin Heidegger, *The Fundamental Concepts of Metaphysics: World, Finitude, Solitude*, trans. William McNeill and Nicholas Walker (Bloomington: Indiana University Press, 1995), 197.

12. On the anthropological tradition, see Tim Ingold's discussion of what he calls "the building perspective" influenced by Clifford Geertz's "assertion that culture—or at least that kind of culture taken to be the hallmark of humanity—consists in 'the imposition of an arbitrary framework of symbolic meaning upon reality.'" Tim Ingold, *The Perception of the Environment: Essays on Livelihood, Dwelling, and Skill* (New York: Routledge, 2000), 178. On the participation of animals in the transmission of culture, see Frans de Waal, *Ape and the Sushi Master: Cultural Reflections by a Primatologist* (New York: Basic Books, 2001), and the discussion in Erica Fudge, *Animal* (London: Reaction Books, 2002), 133–134.

13. J. M. Coetzee, *The Lives of Animals* (Princeton, N.J.: Princeton University Press, 1999), 23.

14. Jakob von Uexküll, *A Foray Into the Worlds of Animals and Humans*, trans. Joseph D. O'Neil (Minneapolis: University of Minnesota Press, 2010), 42.

15. In the use of the pronoun *it* as translation of the gendered pronouns demanded by the German, we already see a problem that might not be apparent in the original. Do we ascribe subjectivity to an "it' or only to a "he" or a "she"? To what extent is a legible gender a defining aspect of subjectivity?

16. Uexküll, *A Foray*, 94.

17. Ibid., 43.

18. Ibid., 50.

19. Jacques Derrida, *Of Spirit*, trans. Geoffrey Bennington and Rachel Bowlby (Chicago: University of Chicago Press, 1989), 49.

20. Derrida, *The Animal*, 48.

21. The fantasy continues even among postmodernists such as Rosi Braidotti, who asks, "What if consciousness were an inferior mode of relating to one's environment and to others . . . no cognitively or morally different from the pathetic howling of wolves in full moonlight. What if, by comparison with the know-how of animals, conscious self-representation were blighted by narcissistic delusions and consequently blinded by its own aspirations to self-transparency." Rosi Braidotti, "Between the No Longer and the Not Yet: Nomadic Variations on the Body," available at http://www.women .it/4thfemconf/lunapark/braidotti.htm.

22. Jean-Jacques Rousseau, *Reveries of the Solitary Walker*, trans. Peter France (New York: Penguin, 1979), 86–87.

23. Rainer Maria Rilke, "The Eighth Elegy," in *The Selected Poetry of Rainer Maria Rilke*, ed. and trans. Stephen Mitchell (New York: Vintage, 1989), 193.

24. Eric L. Santner, *On Creaturely Life* (Chicago: Chicago University Press, 2005), 8, emphasis in original.

25. In his reading of Heidegger, Matthew Calarco gives a concise definition of anthropocentrism as "simply the dominant tendency within the Western Metaphysical tradition to determine the essence of animal life by the measure of, and in opposition to the human." Matthew Calarco, "Heidegger's Zoontology," in Peter Atterton and Matthew Calarco, eds., *Animal Philosophy* (London: Continuum, 2004), 29.

26. Giorgio Agamben, *The Open: Man and Animal* (Stanford, Calif.: Stanford University Press, 2002), 65, italics in original.

27. Heidegger, *The Fundamental Concepts of Physics*, 255.

28. Ibid., 65.

29. David Ross, "Foreword," in David Ross, Bill Viola, Lewis Hyde, and Kira Perov, *Bill Viola* (New York: Whitney Museum of Art, 1997), 25.

30. Quoted in ibid., 28.

31. Heidegger, *The Fundamental Concepts of Physics*, 79.

32. Ingold, *The Perception of the Environment*, 186–187.

33. Quoted in ibid., 186, emphasis in original. Ingold takes the inseparability of dwelling and building further than Heidegger, who would restrict building to "world forming" and thus to humans. For Ingold, animals, too, are builders who adapt to environments fashioned by their forbears and develop specific "skills, sensibilities and dispositions" (186) within those environments.

34. Catherine Russell, "Subjectivity Lost and Found: Bill Viola's 'I Do Not Know What It Is I Am Like,'" in Barry Keith Grant and Jeannette Sloniowski, eds., *Documenting the Documentary* (Detroit: Wayne State University Press, 1998), 356.

35. Rilke, "The Eighth Elegy," 193.

36. According to Michel de Certeau, the writing of history depends on a corpse. See Michel de Certeau, *The Writing of History*, trans. Tom Conley (New York: Columbia University Press, 1988), especially the introduction and chapter 1.

37. Jacques Lacan, "The Mirror Stage," in *Écrits: A Selection*, trans. Alan Sheridan (New York: Norton, 1977), 4.

38. Ibid., 1.

39. John Berger, "Why Look at Animals," in *About Looking* (New York: Vintage Books, 1980), 28.

40. Ibid.

41. Rilke, "The Black Cat," in *Selected Poetry*, 65.

42. Rilke, "The Eighth Elegy," 193.

43. Martin Heidegger, "The Age of the World Picture," in *The Question Concerning Technology and Other Essays*, trans. William Lovitt (New York: Harper Colophon Books, 1977), 129.

44. Ibid., 128.

45. Russell, "Subjectivity Lost and Found," 348.

46. Ibid., 352.

47. Agamben, *The Open*, 27.

48. Ibid., 37.

49. Ibid., 62.

50. Such a project of letting be is envisioned as the endpoint of Agamben's own hope for history insofar as it provides a means of bringing the anthropological machine to a standstill. "To let the animal be would then mean: to let it be *outside of being*. . . . But what is thus left to be outside of being is not thereby negated or taken away; it is not, for this reason inexistent. It is an existing, real thing that has gone beyond the difference between being and beings." Ibid., 91–92, emphasis in original.

51. Maurice Merleau-Ponty, "Eye and Mind," in *The Primacy of Perception*, trans. Carleton Dallery (Evanston, Ill.: Northwestern University Press, 1964), 162, quoted in Ingold, *The Perception of the Environment*, 263.

52. Frans de Waal, "Anthropomorphism and Anthropodenial," in *Primates and Philosophers* (Princeton, N.J.: Princeton University Press, 2006), 5.

53. Rilke, "The Panther," in *Selected Poetry*, 25.

54. Berger, "Why Look at Animals," 28.

55. Steve Baker, *Picturing the Beast* (Urbana: University of Illinois Press, 2001), 221.

56. See, for instance , Lorraine Daston and Gregg Mitman, "Introduction: The How and Why of Thinking with Animals," in Lorraine Daston and Gregg Mitman, eds., *Thinking with Animals: New Perspectives on Anthropomorphism*, 1–14 (New York: Columbia University Press, 2005).

57. Chimp Portraits was on view in conjunction with Who's Looking: A Collaborative, Multi-Disciplinary Investigation of Human Relations to Chimpanzees, an exhibition organized by Lori Gruen at Wesleyan University, November 3 to December 2, 2007.

3. Is a Pet an Animal?

1. Erica Fudge, *Animal* (London: Reaction Books, 2002), 27.

2. Gilles Deleuze and Félix Guattari, *A Thousand Plateaus: Capitalism and Schizophrenia*, trans. Brian Massumi (Minneapolis: University of Minnesota Press, 1987), 240.

3. Ibid., 240.

4. Ibid., 241.

5. Ibid.

6. John Berger, "Why Look at Animals," in *About Looking* (New York: Vintage, 1992), 14.

7. Kathleen Kete, *The Beast in the Boudoir: Pet Keeping in Nineteenth-Century Paris* (Berkeley and Los Angeles: University of California Press, 1995), 95.

8. Harriet Ritvo, *The Animal Estate* (Cambridge, Mass.: Harvard University Press, 1987), 115.

9. Yi-Fu Tuan, *Dominance and Affection: The Making of Pets* (New Haven, Conn.: Yale University Press, 1984), 2.

10. Ibid., 176.

11. Juliet Clutton-Brock, "The Unnatural World: Behavioral Aspects of Humans and Animals in the Process of Domestication," in Aubrey Manning and James Serpell, eds., *Animals and Human Society* (London: Routledge, 1994), 26.

12. Ritvo, *The Animal Estate*, 15–16.

13. Richard Bulliet, *Hunters, Herders, and Hamburgers* (New York: Columbia University Press, 2005), 43.

14. Jean-Jacques Rousseau, "Discourse on the Origin and Foundations of Inequality Among Men," in *The Discourses and Other Early Political Writings*,

ed. and trans. Victor Gourevitch (Cambridge, U.K.: Cambridge University Press, 1997), 138–139.

15. Ibid., 141, 212.

16. Steven Budiansky, *The Covenant of the Wild: Why Animals Chose Domestication* (New Haven, Conn.: Yale University Press, 1999).

17. Philip Armstrong, *What Animals Mean in the Fiction of Modernity* (London: Routledge, 2008), 3. See also Chris Philo and Chris Wilbert, "Animal Spaces, Beastly Places: An Introduction," in Chris Philo and Chris Wilbert, eds., *Animal Spaces, Beastly Places: New Geographies of Human–Animal Relations* (London: Routledge, 2000), and the discussion in Jonathan Burt, *Animals in Film* (London: Reaction Books, 2002), 31.

18. Bulliet, *Hunters, Herders, and Hamburgers*, 46.

19. Ibid.

20. See Rebecca Cassidy, "Introduction," in Rebecca Cassidy and Molly Mullin, eds., *Where the Wild Things Are Now: Domestication Reconsidered* (Oxford, U.K.: Berg, 2007), 7.

21. Donna Haraway writes that " co-constitutive companion species and co-evolution are the rule, not the exception." Donna Haraway, *When Species Meet* (Minneapolis: University of Minnesota Press, 2008), 220. See her various references to Lynn Margulis's theory of "symbiogenesis" and to coevolution in this same work (31–33).

22. On domestication from anthropological perspectives, see Cassidy and Mullin, eds., *Where the Wild Things Are Now*.

23. Frans de Waal, *Primates and Philosophers: How Morality Evolved* (Princeton, N.J.: Princeton University Press, 2006), 65.

24. Gala Argent, "Do Clothes Make the Horse? Relationality, Roles, and Statuses in Iron Age Inner Asia," *World Archeology* 42, no. 2 (2010), 162.

25. Keith Thomas, *Man and the Natural World* (New York: Penguin, 1983), chap. 3.

26. Mary Louise Pratt, "Arts of the Contact Zone," in *Ways of Reading*, 5th ed., ed. David Bartholomae and Anthony Petrosky (New York: Bedford and St. Martin's, 1999), 519.

27. Haraway, *When Species Meet*, 220.

28. Cassidy, "Introduction," 12.

29. Deleuze and Guattari, *A Thousand Plateaus*, 241.

30. Burt, *Animals in Film*, 32.

31. Vicki Hearne, *Adam's Task: Calling Animals by Name* (Pleasantville, N.Y.: Akadine Press, 2000), chap. 3 and p. 132.

32. See Carrie Rohman, *Stalking the Subject: Modernism and the Animal* (New York: Columbia University Press, 2009); and Armstrong, *What Animals Mean*.

33. On animals under industrial capitalism, see Berger, "Why Look at Animals," and Armstrong, *What Animals Mean*. On the postdomestic, see Bulliet, *Hunters, Herders, and Hamburgers*. On epistemological shifts with regard to animals, see Keith Tester, *Animals and Society: The Humanity of Animal Rights* (London: Routledge, 1991).

34. Adrian Franklin, *Animals and Modern Cultures* (London: Sage, 1999), 24.

4. Gendered Subjects/Abject Objects

1. Alice Kuzniar, *Melancholia's Dog: Reflections on Our Animal Kinship* (Chicago: University of Chicago Press, 2006), 68.

2. Ibid.

3. Julia Kristeva, *Powers of Horror: An Essay on Abjection*, trans. Leon S. Roudiez (New York: Columbia University Press, 1982), 10.

4. Kelly Oliver, *Animal Lessons: How They Teach Us to Be Human* (New York: Columbia University Press, 2009), 282.

5. Thomas Mann, "Tobias Mindernickel," in *Death in Venice and Other Stories*, trans. Jefferson S. Chase (New York: Penguin, 1999), 1; subsequent citations are given parenthetically in the text.

6. Paul Bishop, "The Intellectual World of Thomas Mann," in Ritchie Robertson, ed., *The Cambridge Companion to Thomas Mann* (Cambridge, U.K.: Cambridge University Press, 2002), 22.

7. Jean-Jacques Rousseau, "Discourse on the Origin and the Foundations of Inequality Among Men," in *The Discourses and Other Early Political Writings*, ed. and trans. Victor Gourevich (Cambridge, U.K.: Cambridge University Press, 1997), 53.

8. Insofar as suffering appears to be the intended rather than unavoidable result of Tobias's actions, he offers a perverse example of Donna Haraway's notion of "shared suffering," whereby lab technicians and others might attempt to feel the pain they inflict as a result of remaining "at risk and in solidarity in instrumental relationships that one does not disavow." Donna Haraway, *When Species Meet* (Minneapolis: University of Minnesota Press, 2008), 70.

9. Compare Michel Foucault, *The History of Sexuality*, vol. 1: *An Introduction*, trans. Robert Hurley (New York: Vintage, 1980), 43, and Susan McHugh,

"Marrying My Bitch: J. R. Ackerly's Pack Sexualities," *Critical Inquiry* 27 (Autumn 2000), 21–22.

10. See Rabbi Judah Elijah Schochet, *Animal Life in Jewish Tradition* (Jersey City: KTAV, 1984). In Deuteronomy 23:19, for example, dogs are identified with male prostitutes—an association worth mentioning with potential relevance to Mann's story.

11. Wesley Chamberlain, *Nietzsche in Turin* (London: Quartet Books, 1996, 208). See also Michael Wood's discussion of the horse episode in his book *Literature and the Taste of Knowledge* (Cambridge, U.K.: Cambridge University Press, 2005), chap. 6.

12. Fyodor Dostoevsky, *Crime and Punishment*, trans. Jessie Coulson (New York: Norton Critical Edition, 1975), 50.

13. Readers may also be reminded of Freud's 1919 essay on sexual fantasy and perversion in which he examines a similar shifting identification between beater and beaten. See Sigmund Freud, "A Child Is Being Beaten," in *The Standard Edition of the Complete Psychological Works of Sigmund Freud*, 2d ed., 17:179–204 (London: Hogarth Press, 1955).

14. Jeremy Bentham, *An Introduction to the Principles of Morals and Legislation*, chap. 17, sec. 1, available at http://www.animal-rights-library.com/texts-c/bentham01.htm.

15. Robert Alter, trans. and commentary, *Genesis* (New York: Norton, 1996), 129 n. 31.

16. Hannelore Mundt, *Understanding Thomas Mann* (Columbia: University of South Carolina Press, 2004), 26.

17. Nietzsche has been known to be in the position of horse, too. See, for example, "Nietzsche Beaten by Salome," *New York Times*, March 26, 2000, available at http://www.nytimes.com/2000/03/26/theater/theater-who-is-that-man-posing-as-richard-foreman.html?pagewanted=2.

18. Friedrich Nietzsche, *The Will to Power*, trans. Walter Kauffman (New York: Vintage, 1968), 199.

19. Roland Barthes, *Camera Lucida*, trans. Richard Howard (New York: Farrar, Straus and Giroux, 1981), 117; see also Jacques Derrida, *The Animal That Therefore I Am*, trans. David Wills, ed. Marie-Louise Mallet (New York: Fordham University Press, 2008), 35.

20. Friedrich Nietzsche, *The Antichrist*, in *The Portable Nietzsche* (New York: Penguin, 1954), 572–573.

21. Pity and empathy are not necessarily the same emotion, but Nietzsche's use of pity has much in common with the kind of empathy that Tobias displays.

22. On empathy in history, see Carolyn Dean, *The Fragility of Empathy After the Holocaust* (Ithaca, N.Y.: Cornell University Press, 2004); Dominick

LaCapra, *Experience, Identity, and Critical Theory* (Ithaca, N.Y.: Cornell University Press, 2004); and Samuel Moyn, "Empathy in History, Empathizing with Humanity," *History and Theory* 45 (October 2006): 397–415. On empathy in animal studies, see Lori Gruen, "Empathy and Vegetarian Commitments," in Josephine Donovan and Carol J. Adams, eds., *The Feminist Care Tradition in Animal Ethics*, 333–343 (New York: Columbia University Press, 2007). Primatologist Frans de Waal's recent book *The Age of Empathy: Nature's Lessons for a Kinder Society* (New York: Harmony Book, 2009) suggests that empathy is both the new theme for our times and a talent that has evolved from our animal origins.

23. Moyn, "Empathy in History," 400.

24. See, for instance, Lori Gruen on what she calls "engaged empathy" in "Attending to Nature: Empathetic Engagement with the More Than Human World," *Ethics and Environment* 14, no. 2 (Fall 2009): 23–38.

25. Kenneth Shapiro, "Understanding Dogs Through Kinesthetic Empathy, Social Construction, and History," *Anthrozoos* 3 (1990): 184–195; Ralph Acampora, "Bodily Being and Animal World: Toward a Somatology of Cross-Species Community," in H. Peter Steeves, ed., *Animal Others: On Ethics, Ontology, and Animal Life* (Albany: State University of New York Press, 1999), 119.

26. Edgar Allen Poe, "The Black Cat," in *The Portable Edgar Allen Poe*, ed. J. Gerald Kennedy (New York: Penguin, 2006), 192.

27. Stanley Cavell, *In Quest of the Ordinary* (Chicago: University of Chicago Press, 1988), 144.

28. Ibid., 137.

29. Guy de Maupassant, "Fou?" in *Contes et nouvelles*, vol. 1, ed. Louis Forestier (Paris: Gallimard, 1974), 525, my translation.

30. Ibid., 526.

31. Cary Wolfe discusses the "logic of the pet" and the status of "humanized animals," which constitute an exception to the sacrificial structure described by Derrida. See Cary Wolfe, *Animal Rites, American Culture: The Discourse of Species and Posthumanist Theory* (Chicago: University of Chicago Press, 2003), 100–101, 104.

32. Carrie Rohman, *Stalking the Subject* (New York: Columbia University Press, 2009), 15.

33. Thomas Mann, *Man and Dog: An Idyll*, in *Death in Venice and Other Stories*, 219–302; subsequent citations are given parenthetically in the text.

34. According to Michael Fischer, "Cavell suggests that happiness, maybe even sanity, depends on being touched by Othello's problems but not done in by them"; see Michael Fischer, *Stanley Cavell and Literary Skepticism* (Chicago: University of Chicago Press, 1989), 87.

35. See, for instance, Hannelore Mundt, *Understanding Thomas Mann* (Columbia: University of South Carolina Press, 2004), 10.

36. Stanley Cavell, *Pursuits of Happiness: The Hollywood Comedy of Remarriage* (Cambridge, Mass.: Harvard University Press, 1981).

37. "It has its point of view regarding me," writes Derrida of his cat. Jacques Derrida, *The Animal That Therefore I Am*, trans. David Wills, ed. Marie-Louise Mallet (New York: Fordham University Press, 2008), 11.

38. Baushan thus resists the growing institutional understanding of dogs according to categories of breed rather than according to the individual. See, for instance, the chapter "Prize Pets," in Harriet Ritvo, *The Animal Estate: The English and Other Creatures in the Victorian Age*, 82–124 (Cambridge, Mass.: Harvard University Press, 1989).

39. Freedom, Rousseau writes in *The Social Contract*, is "obedience to a law which we prescribe to ourselves." Jean-Jacques Rousseau, *The Social Contract*, trans. G. D. H. Cole, book 1, chap. 8, available at http://www.constitution.org/jjr/socon_01.htm#008.

40. Vicki Hearne, *Adam's Task: Calling Animals by Name* (Pleasantville, N.Y.: Akadine Press, 2000), 66.

41. For an elaboration of this sense of abjection, see Kristeva, *Powers of Horror*.

42. As Arnold Arluke and Clinton Saunders discuss in a chapter on animals in Nazi Germany, the wild predator became a model for German Nazi youth, whose task it was to reverse the weakness wrought by domestication. "I want violent, imperious, fearless, cruel young people," wrote Hitler. "The free, magnificent beast of prey must once again flash from their eyes. . . . I shall blot out thousands of years of human domestication. I shall have the pure, noble stuff of nature." Quoted in Arnold Arluke and Clinton Saunders, *Regarding Animals* (Philadelphia: Temple University Press, 1996), 139, 140.

43. Diana Donald discusses the conflicting emotions of the "sporting instinct" and the "blood lust" that "[coexist] with love and veneration for the hunted animal." Diana Donald, "Pangs Watched in Perpetuity," in Animal Studies Group, ed., *Killing Animals* (Urbana: University of Illinois Press, 2006), 50.

44. Quoted in Vanessa Lemm, *Nietzsche's Animal Philosophy* (New York: Fordham University Press, 2009), 10. The first chapter of Lemm's book discusses the importance of this antagonism in relation to Nietzsche's sense of "human animal life": "What defines culture is freedom from moralization, from the 'willed and forced animal taming' of civilization, and from its intolerance toward 'free spirits.' When culture rules over civilization, what rules is the freedom of the animal and of the spirit" (12).

• • • • • • • • • • • •

45. Ibid., 17.

46. Friedrich Nietzsche, *On the Use and Abuse of History*, trans. Adrian Collins (New York: Macmillan, 1957), 5.

47. Ibid., 7.

48. Ibid.

49. On "true" history for Nietzsche or what Lemm calls "artistic historiography," see Lemm, *Nietzsche's Animal Philosophy*, 99–102.

50. See Nietzsche, *On the Use and Abuse of History*, 5. On the silence of Nietzsche's animals, see Lemm, *Nietzsche's Animal Philosophy*, 114–115.

51. "To breed an animal *with the right to make promises*—is not this the paradoxical task that nature has set itself in the case of man? Is it not the real problem regarding man?" Friedrich Nietzsche, "On the Genealogy of Morals," in *On the Genealogy of Morals and Ecce Homo*, trans. and ed. Walter Kaufmann (New York: Vintage, 1969), 57.

5. Dog Love/W(o)olf Love

1. Marjorie Garber, *Dog Love* (New York: Touchstone, 1997).

2. Quoted in Anna Snaith, "Of Fanciers, Footnotes, and Fascism: Virginia Woolf's *Flush*," *Modern Fiction Studies* 48, no. 8 (Fall 2002), 618. As her title indicates, Snaith also connects the writing of *Flush* to political issues raised in *Three Guineas*.

3. Virginia Woolf, *Three Guineas* (New York: Harcourt Brace and World: 1966), 134, 142.

4. As Craig Smith and others have indicated, the initial reception of *Flush* criticized its anthropomorphism as a form of "sentimentalism." See Craig Smith, "Across the Widest Gulf: Nonhuman Subjectivity in Virginia Woolf's *Flush*," *Twentieth Century Literature* 48, no. 3 (Autumn 2002), 351.

5. Kate Flint, "Introduction," in Virginia Woolf, *Flush* (Oxford, U.K.: Oxford University Press, 2009), xiii.

6. Naomi Schor, "This Essentialism Which Is Not One," *differences* 1, no. 2 (1988), 45–46.

7. Frans de Waal, "Appendix A: Anthropomorphism and Anthropodenial," in *Primates and Philosophers: How Morality Evolved*, 59–68 (Princeton, N.J.: Princeton University Press, 2006).

8. On the various animal and creaturely expressions Woolf used to address her friends and family, see Flint, "Introduction," xii.

9. Elizabeth de Fontenay, *Sans offenser le genre humain* (Paris: Albin Michel, 2008), 119, my translation.

10. Virginia Woolf, *A Room of One's Own* (New York: Harcourt Brace, 1981), 99.

11. Woolf, *Flush*, 31; subsequent citations to this work are given parenthetically in the text; ellipses in quotes are mine unless otherwise noted.

12. Woolf, *A Room of One's Own*, 104.

13. Ibid., 113–114.

14. Virginia Woolf, *Orlando* (New York: Harcourt Brace Jovanovich, 1956), 13.

15. Marc Shell, "The Family Pet," *Representations* 15 (Summer 1986): 121–153. Shell is less concerned with the individual pet owner than with understanding how Western familial and national structures affect the institution of pethood—its sexual, familial, and sociopolitical role. As a chaste, safe, and voluntary transgression of kinship boundaries, Woolf's pet love contrasts with the incest she experienced.

16. "Originally the word [*anthropomorphism*] referred to the attribution of human form to gods, forbidden by several religions as blasphemous." Lorraine Daston and Gregg Mitman, "Introduction: The How and Why of Thinking with Animals," in Lorraine Daston and Gregg Mitman, eds., *Thinking with Animals: New Perspectives on Anthropomorphism* (New York: Columbia University Press, 2004), 2.

17. Jacques Lacan, "God and the *Jouissance* of ~~the~~ Woman," in *Feminine Sexuality: Jacques Lacan and the École freudienne*, trans. Jacqueline Rose, ed. Juliet Mitchell and Jacqueline Rose (New York: Norton, 1982), 138.

18. Kari Weil, *Androgyny and the Denial of Difference* (Charlottesville: University of Virginia Press, 1992), esp. 2–11.

19. "Man is an animal, but a speaking one, and he is less a beast of prey than a beast that is prey to language." Jacques Derrida, *The Animal That Therefore I Am*, trans. David Wills, ed. Marie-Louise Mallet (New York: Fordham University Press, 2008), 120–121.

20. Susan Squier, *Virginia Woolf and London: The Sexual Politics of the City* (Chapel Hill: University of North Carolina Press, 1985). Squier devotes a whole chapter to *Flush*.

21. Charles Darwin, *The Descent of Man* (New York: Penguin Books, 2004), 680.

22. Sigmund Freud, *Civilization and Its Discontents*, in *The Standard Edition of the Complete Psychological Works of Sigmund Freud* (London: Hogarth Press, 1978), 21:89.

23. Ibid., 21:111.

24. Quoted in Paul Guyer, *Kant on Freedom, Law, and Happiness* (Cambridge, U.K.: Cambridge University Press, 2000), 152.

25. Freud, *Civilization and Its Discontents*, 21:11.

26. Finding an alternative to this either/or condition of submission to a dominant authority or the unleashing of so-called animal instincts had clear, political urgency in Europe in 1933, as it already had for Thomas Mann some years earlier.

27. Freud, *Civilization and Its Discontents*, 21:110.

28. Wolfgang M. Schleidt and Michael D. Shalter, "Co-Evolution of Humans and Canids: An Alternative View of Dog Domestication: Homo Homini Lupus?" *Evolution and Cognition* 9, no. 1 (2003), 60.

29. Ibid., 62.

30. Squier, *Virginia Woolf and London*, 128.

31. Anna Snaith argues that *Flush* needs to be understood within the politics of the 1930s and contemporary fears about the growth of fascism. Anna Snaith, "Of Fanciers, Footnotes, and Fascism: Virginia Woolf's *Flush*," *Modern Fiction Studies* 48, no. 3 (2002): 614–636.

32. Freud, *Civilization and Its Discontents*, 21:103. In this respect, Woolf understands dog obedience differently than Vicki Hearne, who argues that dogs work less for love than for "coherent authority." See Vicki Hearne, *Adam's Task: Calling Animals by Name* (Pleasantville, N.Y.: Akadine Press, 2000), specifically "How to Say, 'Fetch!'" 42–76.

33. Woolf, *Three Guineas*, 109.

34. Freud, *Civilization and Its Discontents*, 21:99–100 n. 1.

35. Quoted in Todd Dufresne, *Killing Freud: Twentieth-Century Culture and the Death of Psychoanalysis* (New York: Continuum, 2003), 146.

36. Alice Kuzniar, *Melancholia's Dog: Reflections on Our Animal Kinship* (Chicago: University of Chicago Press, 2006), 72.

37. Jean-Paul Sartre, *Being and Nothingness*, trans. Hazel Estella Barnes (New York: Simon and Schuster, 1985), 302.

38. Dufresne, *Killing Freud*, 147.

39. Ibid.; see also Garber, *Dog Love*, 249.

40. Woolf, *A Room of One's Own*, 84.

6. A Proper Death

1. Richard Klein, "The Power of Pets," *The New Republic*, July 10, 1995, 23.

2. Virginia Woolf, *Flush: A Biography* (Oxford, U.K.: Oxford University Press, 2009), 105–106.

3. Leo Tolstoy, "Strider: The Story of a Horse," in Steven D. Price, ed., *Classic Horse Stories* (Guilford, Conn.: Lyons Press, 2002), 274.

• • • • • • • • • • • •

4. Quoted in Jacques Derrida, *Aporias*, trans. Thomas Dutoit (Stanford, Calif.: Stanford University Press, 1993), 35.

5. Hélène Cixous, "Castration or Decapitation," in Kelly Oliver, ed., *French Feminism Reader* (New York: Rowman and Littlefield, 2000), 284.

6. For a provocative discussion of dog death in Victorian literature, see Ivan Kreilkamp, "Dying Like a Dog in *Great Expectations*," in Deborah Morse and Martin Danahay, eds., *Animal Dreams: Representations of Animals in Victorian Literature and Culture*, 81–94 (Burlington, Vt.: Ashgate, 2007).

7. Jean-Jacques Rousseau, "On the Origin and the Foundations of Inequality Among Men," in *The Discourses and Other Early Political Writings*, ed. and trans. Victor Gourevitch (Cambridge, U.K.: Cambridge University Press, 1997), 142.

8. Tolstoy, "Strider," 272.

9. Walter Benjamin, "On Language as Such and on the Language of Man," in *Reflections*, ed. Peter Demetz (New York: Harcourt Brace Jovanovich, 1978), 330.

10. Georges Bataille, *The Tears of Eros*, trans. Peter Conner (San Francisco: City Lights, 2001), 52.

11. Ibid., 53.

12. Georges Bataille, "Animality," in Peter Atterton and Matthew Calarco, eds., *Animal Philosophy* (London: Continuum, 2004), 34.

13. Bataille, *The Tears of Eros*, 45.

14. Derrida, *Aporias*, 6.

15. Steve Baker, "Animal Death in Contemporary Art," in Animal Studies Group, ed., *Killing Animals* (Urbana: University of Illinois Press, 2006), 83. See also Steve Baker, *The Postmodern Animal* (London: Reaction Books, 2000).

16. Baker, *The Postmodern Animal*, 8.

17. Taylor-Wood's "little death" is itself an aporia between life and death and between animal and human death as defined by Heidegger. Heidegger says that animals perish and thus come to an end, but he reserves for man a death that, as Derrida explains, is "without end." "Even if it dies (*stirbt*) and even if it ends (*endet*), it never 'kicks the bucket' (*verendet nie*)" (Derrida, *Aporias*, 40). This "little death" appears to be without end, but it also appears to be animal.

18. As an effect of a body's dissolution, the liveness of Taylor-Wood's hare is thus different from the "enlivening effect of bodily presence" that Baker describes in reference to a display of taxidermic polar bears and that, he argues, contributes to a new, physical history of the animal. See Steve Baker, "What Can Dead Bodies Do?" in Bryndis Snaebjornsdottir and Mark Wilson,

eds., *Nanoq: Flat Out and Bluesome: A Cultural Life of Polar Bears* (London: Black Dog, 2006), 152.

19. Baker, "Animal Death," 74.

20. Dominick LaCapra, *History and Its Limits: Human, Animal Violence* (Ithaca, N.Y.: Cornell University Press, 2009), 7.

21. Ibid., 170.

22. Of course, even before Woolf's biography, Flush lived on in the poems written about him by Elizabeth Barrett Browning. As for Tolstoy, he is estimated to have spent seven years of his life in the saddle, and the impact of horses generally on his life is summed up by an anecdote Turgenev told of overhearing him talking to a horse along the road. "I could not refrain from remarking," Turgenev later wrote, "beyond any doubt you must have been a horse once yourself." Quoted in Price, "Introduction," in Price, ed., *Classic Horse Stories*, 5.

23. Taylor-Wood thus reverses the sublimity of death and "livingness" discussed by Edmund Burke in his essay on the sublime, where, as Jonathan Burt writes, the "striking" quality of death allows us to overlook or "take for granted" the "state of livingness." In Taylor-Wood's video, on the contrary, livingness is striking and mesmerizing also because of its duration. See Jonathan Burt, "Derrida, Bergson, Deleuze, and Animal Film Imagery," *Configurations* 14, nos. 1–2 (Winter–Spring 2006), 167.

24. Sigmund Freud, "Mourning and Melancholia" (1917), in *The Standard Edition of the Complete Psychological Works of Sigmund Freud*, trans. and ed. James Strachey, 14:239–260 (London: Hogarth Press, 1961).

25. Baker suggests that the attitudes and practices he discusses might provisionally be said to tend toward either the melancholic or the mournful. But I disagree with his characterization of melancholia as conservative because it "clings to certainties" (Baker, *Postmodern Animal*, 164). I would say rather that melancholia's potential conservatism comes from its clinging to ambivalence for its own sake.

26. Gilles Deleuze and Félix Guattari, "Becoming Animal," in Atterton and Calarco, eds., *Animal Philosophy*, 87–100.

27. Quoted in Steve Baker, "What Does Becoming-Animal Look Like?" in Nigel Rothfels, ed., *Representing Animals* (Bloomington: Indiana University Press, 2002), 67.

28. Dominick LaCapra, *Writing History, Writing Trauma* (Baltimore: Johns Hopkins University Press, 2001), 22.

29. Hélène Cixous, "Shared at Dawn," in *Stigmata: Escaping Texts* (London: Routledge, 1998), 177.

30. Gilles Deleuze [and Félix Guattari], "Becoming Animal," in *The Deleuze Reader*, ed. Constantin V. Boundas (New York: Columbia University Press, 1993), 122.

31. Derrida, *Aporias*, 34.

32. Cixous, "Shared at Dawn," 176.

33. Ibid., 179.

34. Freud, "Mourning and Melancholia," 14:245.

35. Judith Butler, *Gender Trouble* (New York: Routledge, 1990), 63. See also Judith Butler, "Melancholy Gender—Refused Identification," *Psychoanalytic Dialogues* 5, no. 2 (1995): 165–180.

36. Cixous, "Shared at Dawn," 176.

37. Another avenue for pursuing this connection is through Julia Kristeva's notion of abjection as a disavowal of our primary dependence on and connection to our mother as to other animals. Abjection is similar to melancholia in that it is a state that holds onto even as it attempts to separate from an "object" that is not yet an object because it is unrepresented. As Kelly Oliver writes, "Abjection is the constant attempt and constant failure, to separate from the primary 'object,' which is the (or an) animal on the level of society and the (or a) mother on the level of personal archaeology." Kelly Oliver, *Animal Lessons: How They Teach Us to Be Human* (New York: Columbia University Press, 2009), 282.

38. Luce Irigaray, *Speculum of the Other Woman*, trans. Gillian C. Gill (Ithaca, N.Y.: Cornell University Press, 1974), 68.

39. Cixous, "Castration or Decapitation," 288, emphasis in original.

40. Butler, *Gender Trouble*, 68.

41. Cixous, "Castration or Decapitation," 288.

42. Judith Butler, *Precarious Life: The Powers of Mourning and Violence* (London: Verso, 2004), 27, 28.

43. "Introduction," in Animal Studies Group, ed., *Killing Animals*, 3, my ellipses in brackets.

44. Butler, *Precarious Life*, xviii–xix.

45. Ibid., 36.

46. Chloe Taylor, "The Precarious Lives of Animals," *Philosophy Today* 52, no. 1 (2008), 3.

47. Ibid.

48. Charles Patterson notes this exemption in *Eternal Treblinka: Our Treatment of Animals and the Holocaust* (New York: Lantern Books, 2002), 71, cited in LaCapra, *History and Its Limits*, 179.

49. Butler, *Precarious Life*, 36. The state of the semiliving or undead brings to mind the laboratory tick discussed by the biologist Jakob von Uexküll; the

tick was artificially isolated from its environment and kept "in a sleep-like state" and withheld nourishment for eighteen years. It was an object of fascination for Giorgio Agamben, as it was perhaps for von Uexküll, but neither considers the ethics of such treatment. Who cares about a tick?

50. Marjorie Garber, "Reflections," in J. M. Coetzee, *The Lives of Animals*, 73–84 (Princeton, N.J.: Princeton University Press, 2001).

51. Butler, *Precarious Life*, 22.

52. LaCapra, *History and Its Limits*, 186 n. 49. LaCapra criticizes Cary Wolfe and to a certain extent Derrida for overvaluing passivity and disempowerment.

53. Well, we all have to eat, Derrida might remind us.

54. Butler, *Precarious Life*, 23.

7. Thinking and Unthinking Animal Death

1. On this distinction, see Beatrice Hanssen, "Ethics of the Other," in Marjorie Garber, Beatrice Hanssen, and Rebecca L. Walkowitz, eds., *The Turn to Ethics* (New York: Routledge, 2000), 134–135.

2. Donna J. Haraway, *When Species Meet* (Minneapolis: University of Minnesota Press, 2008), 79–80.

3. Jacques Derrida, "'Eating Well' or the Calculation of the Subject," in Elizabeth Weber, ed., *Points . . . Interviews 1974–1994*, trans. Peggy Kamuf and others, 255–287 (Stanford, Calif.: Stanford University Press, 1995).

4. Haraway, *When Species Meet*, 81.

5. Derrida, "'Eating Well,'" 273.

6. Both Derrida and Haraway build on even while deconstructing or transgressing the distinction that Lacan makes between an animal's instinctive or mechanical "reaction" and a human's ability to "respond." To respond, in other words, is to act out of the freedom to choose and with understanding of the repercussions of various choices. We humans cannot always be sure when our so-called responses are merely reactions.

7. Cora Diamond, "The Difficulty of Reality and the Difficulty of Philosophy," in Stanley Cavell, Cora Diamond, John McDowell, Ian Hacking, and Carey Wolfe, *Philosophy and & Animal Life* (New York: Columbia University Press, 2008), 74, 45–46.

8. Temple Grandin, *Thinking in Pictures and Other Reports from My Life with Autism* (New York: Vintage Books, 1995), 159. In his *Second Discourse*, Rousseau makes a similar comment regarding thinking in pictures or "imaging" as a limited form of thought that can take hold only of the particular

rather than of the general or abstract. See Jean-Jacques Rousseau, "On the Origin and the Foundations of Inequality Among Men," in *The Discourses and Other Early Political Writings*, ed. and trans. Victor Gourevitch (Cambridge, U.K.: Cambridge University Press, 1997), 148.

9. See also Cary Wolfe's discussion of the way Grandin turns her disability into a special ability in "Learning from Temple Grandin," in *What Is Posthumanism?* 127–142 (Minneapolis: University of Minnesota Press, 2010).

10. Temple Grandin, *Animals in Translation: Using the Mysteries of Autism to Decode Animal Behavior* (New York: Scribner, 2005), 65.

11. On this point, see also Cary Wolfe, "Exposures," the introduction to Cavell et al., *Philosophy & Animal Life*, 8.

12. Rainer Maria Rilke, "The Eighth Elegy," in *Duino Elegies*, trans. J. B. Leishman and Stephen Spender (New York: Norton, 1963), 67.

13. J. M. Coetzee, *The Lives of Animals* (Princeton, N.J.: Princeton University Press), 23.

14. Ibid., 51.

15. Jacques Derrida, *The Animal That Therefore I Am*, trans. David Wills, ed., Marie-Louise Mallet (New York: Fordham University Press, 2008), 121.

16. Ibid., 48.

17. Quoted in Jacques Derrida, *Aporias*, trans. Thomas Dutoit (Stanford, Calif.: Stanford University Press, 1993), 35.

18. Rilke, "The Eighth Elegy," 69.

19. John Berger, "Why Look at Animals," in *About Looking*, 3–28 (New York: Vintage, 1992).

20. Indeed, misguided nostalgia for this look has sent celebrity chefs in search of "looking dinner in the eye." See Julia Moskin, "Chefs New Goal: Looking Dinner in the Eye," *New York Times*, January 16, 2008.

21. "Conclusion: A Conversation," in Animal Studies Group, ed., *Killing Animals* (Urbana: University of Illinois Press, 2006), 209.

22. Grandin, *Thinking in Pictures*, 41–42.

23. Wolfe makes similar remarks about this passage and suggests other potential readings in "Learning from Temple Grandin."

24. Grandin, *Thinking in Pictures*, 205.

25. J. M. Coetzee, *Disgrace* (New York: Penguin, 1999), 12; subsequent citations to this work are given parenthetically in the text.

26. Giorgio Agamben, *The Open: Man and Animal*, trans. Kevin Attell (Stanford, Calif.: Stanford University Press, 2004).

27. Ibid., 62.

28. Derrida, *The Animal*, 121.

29. This is the last line of Rilke's poem "Archaic Torso of Apollo," which describes how in the absence of a head "there is no place that does not see you, / You must change your life." In *Selected Poetry of Rainer Maria Rilke*, trans. Stephen Mitchell (New York: Vintage, 1982), 61.

30. Emmanuel Levinas is equivocal at best about an animal's ability to call a human to his or her ethical responsibility. See, for instance, Emmanuel Levinas, "The Name of a Dog, or Natural Rights," in Peter Atterton and Matthew Calarco, eds., *Animal Philosophy*, 47–51 (London: Continuum, 2004).

31. Grandin, *Thinking in Pictures*, 206.

32. Friedrich Nietzsche, *The Gay Science*, trans. Walter Kaufmann (New York: Vintage Books, 1974), 210.

8. Animal Liberation or Shameless Freedom

1. "Conclusion: A Conversation," in Animal Studies Group, ed., *Killing Animals* (Urbana: University of Illinois Press, 2006), 203, 207.

2. Ibid., 205.

3. Matthew Scully, *Dominion: The Power of Man, the Suffering of Animals* (New York: St. Martin's Press, 2002).

4. Ibid., 12.

5. Gary Francione, whom I discuss later in this chapter, is the major representative of the "abolitionist approach," whose mission statement can be read at http://www.abolitionistapproach.com.

6. Donna Haraway, *When Species Meet* (Minneapolis: University of Minnesota Press, 2008), 11. Gala Argent makes similar arguments about human–horse relations. See Gala Argent, "Do Clothes Make the Horse? Relationality, Roles, and Statuses in Asia," *World Archeology* 42, no. 2 (2010): 157–174.

7. Jacques Derrida, *The Beast and the Sovereign*, vol. 1, trans. Geoffrey Bennington (Chicago: University of Chicago Press, 2009), 25.

8. Ibid., 159. The closest English equivalent for the term *bêtise*, meaning simply "stupid" but derived from the word for "beast" or "animal," may be *asinine* because it contains the bestial or animal reference. Derrida's text focuses attention on the gendering of *le souverain* versus *la bête* in ways that recall his discussion of "carnivorous virility" and the gendering of power in "'Eating Well' or the Calculation of the Subject," in Elizabeth Weber, ed., *Points . . . Interviews 1974–1994*, trans. Peggy Kamuf and others (Stanford, Calif.: Stanford University Press, 1995), 280.

9. Gilles Deleuze, *Difference and Repetition*, trans. Paul Patton (New York:

Columbia University Press, 1994), 151, quoted in Derrida, *The Beast and the Sovereign*, 156.

10. Derrida, *The Beast and the Sovereign*, 161.

11. Franz Kafka, "A Report to an Academy," in *Collected Stories*, ed. Gabriel Josipovici (New York: Knopf, 1993), 198.

12. Derrida, *The Beast and the Sovereign*, 157.

13. J. M. Coetzee, *Disgrace* (New York: Penguin, 1999), 215, 220; subsequent citations are given parenthetically in the text.

14. Ian Hacking, "Our Fellow Animals," *New York Review of Books*, June 29, 2000.

15. Josephine Donovan, "'Miracles of Creation': Animals in J. M. Coetzee's Work," *Michigan Quarterly Review* 43, no. 1 (Winter 2004), 79 n. 16.

16. David Attridge, "Age of Bronze, State of Grace: Music and Dogs in Coetzee's *Disgrace*," *Novel* 34 (2000), 115.

17. Louis Tremaine, "The Embodied Soul: Animal Being in the Work of J. M. Coetzee," *Contemporary Literature* 44, no. 4 (2003), 603.

18. Gary Francione, "Animal Welfare and the Moral Value of Nonhuman Animals," paper presented for the monthly meeting of the Animal Ethics Group, Yale University Interdisciplinary Center for Bioethics, New Haven, Conn., December 4, 2008, 1. Francione' s major discussion of the abolitionist position can be found in his book *Rain Without Thunder: The Ideology of the Animal Rights Movement* (Philadelphia: Temple University Press, 2000).

19. Francione, "Animal Welfare," 21.

20. Kari Weil, "Killing Them Softly: Animal Death, Linguistic Disability, and the Struggle for Ethics," *Configurations* 14, no. 1 (2006): 87–96.

21. Although I agree with Donovan's reading in terms of a conversion because I still see that conversion in terms of ideas, my reading is closest to Attridge's and to a lesser extent to Tremaine's, the latter suggesting that Lurie's coming to terms with death and suffering is not primarily intersubjective; rather, "it is one for the self in itself" (Tremaine, "The Embodied Soul," 609). In other words, the particular relationship that exists between Lurie and the dog is irrelevant to his transformation.

22. Tim Ingold, *The Perception of the Environment: Essays on Livelihood, Dwelling, and Skill* (London: Routledge, 2000), 61, emphasis in original.

23. This scenario might be a third to add to the two Heideggerean scenarios of the end of history that Giorgio Agamben describes in *The Open*. In the first scenario, animality is offered up to be governed "by means of technology"; in the second, animality is regarded not as something to be governed or mastered or as something hidden, but rather is "thought as such, as pure abandonment" (Giorgio Agamben, *The Open: Man and Animal*, trans. Kevin

Attell [Stanford, Calif.: Stanford University Press, 2004], 80). In this third, animality is destroyed with the extinction of animals.

24. On recent views regarding the history of domestication, see Rebecca Cassidy and Molly Mullin, eds., *Where the Wild Things Are: Domestication Reconsidered* (Oxford, U.K.: Berg, 2007).

25. On Margulis and the implications of her work on symbiogenesis, see Haraway, *When Species Meet*, 30–33.

26. Ibid., 11.

27. Stacy Alaimo, "Transcorporeal Feminisms and the Ethical Space of Nature," in Stacy Alaimo and Susan Hekman, eds., *Material Feminisms* (Bloomington: Indiana University Press, 2008), 251. On this point, see also Lynda Birke and Luciana Parisi, "Animals Becoming," in H. Peter Steeves, ed., *Animal Others: On Ethics, Ontology, and Animal Life*, 55–73 (Albany: State University of New York Press, 1999).

28. I use the term *abjection* in the sense of casting off or attempting to separate oneself from those natural elements of feces or blood or milk that are seen to defile the self and that are associated with the maternal–feminine. For an elaboration of this meaning of *abjection*, see Julia Kristeva, *Powers of Horror: An Essay on Abjection*, trans. Leon S. Roudiez (New York: Columbia University Press, 1982), esp. chap. 3.

29. Karen Barad, *Meeting the Universe Halfway: Quantum Physics and the Entanglement of Matter and Meaning* (Chapel Hill, N.C.: Duke University Press, 2007).

30. Stacy Alaimo and Susan Hekman, "Introduction: Emerging Models of Materiality in Feminist Theory," in Alaimo and Hekman, eds., *Material Feminisms*, 7.

31. Tremaine foregrounds such a kinship of shameful bodies but without really questioning the meaning or status of shame. See Tremaine, "The Embodied Soul."

32. Alice Kuzniar, *Melancholia's Dog: Reflections on Our Animal Kinship* (Chicago: University of Chicago Press, 2006), 179.

33. Josephine Donovan and Carol Adams, "Introduction," in Josephine Donovan and Carol Adams, eds., *The Feminist Care Tradition in Animal Ethics* (New York: Columbia University Press, 2007), 15.

34. Lori Gruen, for instance, writes of the importance of the empathic person as having a "distinct self . . . so when she is imaginatively engaging with the other, she doesn't believe herself to be in the other's situation." Lori Gruen, "Empathy and Vegetarian Commitments," in Donovan and Adams, eds., *The Feminist Care Tradition*, 337.

35. See Simone Weil, "Reflections on the Right Use of Social Studies with a

View to the Love of God," in *The Simone Weil Reader*, ed. George A. Panichas (New York: McKay, 1977).

36. Kuzniar, *Melancholia's Dog*, 117.

37. Donovan and Adams, "Introduction," 14. In chapter 13 of *The Expression of the Emotions in Man and Animals* (Chicago: University of Chicago Press, 1965), Charles Darwin focuses on the act of "blushing," "the most peculiar and the most human of all expressions," which is caused by shame (309).

38. Quoted in Ruth Leys, *From Guilt to Shame: Auschwitz and After* (Princeton, N.J.: Princeton University Press, 2007), 172.

39. Haraway, *When Species Meet*, 73.

40. It should be stressed that this view can be especially risky for those who are already marginalized.

41. Vicki Hearne, "Job's Animals," in *Animal Happiness: A Moving Exploration of Animals and Their Emotions* (New York: Skyhorse, 1994), 237, 229.

42. Haraway, *When Species Meet*, 36.

43. Hearne, "Job's Animals," 238.

44. In Derrida's essay *The Animal That Therefore I Am*, uprightness concerns not only the human stance, but also, through its association with erection, the sign of masculine power and authority. Jacques Derrida, *The Animal That Therefore I Am*, trans. David Wills, ed. Marie-Louise Mallet (New York: Fordham University Press, 2008).

45. Quoted in Hearne, "Job's Animals," 237.

46. Like Haraway, Hearne thinks of relationships with animals in terms of work, not of use.

47. Attridge says something similar when he writes that Lurie dedicates himself to "the singularity of every living and dead being." Attridge, "Age of Bronze," 117.

48. Judith Butler, *Precarious Life: The Powers of Mourning and Violence* (London: Verso, 2004), 20.

"And Toto Too"

1. L. Frank Baum, *The Wonderful Wizard of Oz* (New York: Modern Library, 2003), 7.

2. Cary Wolfe, *What Is Posthumanism?* (Minneapolis: University of Minnesota Press, 2010), xxv.

3. Emilie Hache and Bruno Latour, "Morality or Moralism? An Exercise in Sensitization," trans. Patrick Camilier, *Common Knowledge* 16, no. 2 (Spring 2010), 2.

. . . .

4. Ibid, 6.

5. Such a view is at the core of Bruno Latour's earlier work *We Have Never Been Modern*, trans. Catherine Porter (Cambridge, Mass.: Harvard University Press, 1993).

6. Priscilla Patton, "Theory: Gone to the Dogs," *JAC* 30, nos. 3–4 (2010), 574, emphasis in original.

7. Elizabeth de Fontenay, *Sans offenser le genre humain* (Paris: Albin Michel, 2008), 119, my translation.

8. Elizabeth de Fontenay, *Le silence des bêtes* (Paris: Fayard, 2006), 703, my translation.

INDEX